THE HISTORY OF
THE BLACK CHURCH

THE HISTORY OF
THE BLACK CHURCH

WITHDRAWN

Norma Jean Lutz

CHELSEA HOUSE PUBLISHERS
Philadelphia

Dedicated to the rich heritage of faith, love,
endurance, and persistence of Black Churches
nationwide. May they continually be blessed.

Chelsea House Publishers
Editor in Chief Sally Cheney
Production Manager Pamela Loos
Picture Editor Judy Hasday
Art Director Sara Davis
Managing Editor James D. Gallagher
Senior Production Editor J. Christopher Higgins

Staff for THE HISTORY OF THE BLACK CHURCH
Associate Art Director Takeshi Takahashi
Designer Keith Trego
Picture Researcher Sandy Jones
Cover Designer Sara Davis

Front Cover Photo: Hosanna Meeting House, at Lincoln University, Pa. Organized by free blacks in 1843, the church was a stop
on the Underground Railroad. It was visited by Frederick
Douglass and Sojourner Truth.

First Printing
1 3 5 7 9 8 6 4 2

The Chelsea House World Wide Web address is
http://www.chelseahouse.com

Library of Congress Cataloging-in-Publication Data

Lutz, Norma Jean.
The History of the Black Church / Norma Jean Lutz.
 p. cm. — (African-American achievers)
Includes bibliographical references and index.
ISBN 0-7910-5822-0 (alk. paper)
1. Afro-American churches—History—juvenile literature.
[1. Afro-Americans—History. 2. Afro-Americans—Religion.]
I. Title. II. Series.
BR563.N4 L88 2000
277.3'0089'96073—dc21   00-045156

Frontispiece: *Christianity has
long been an important element
of African-American life, and
church leaders have ranged
from world leaders like the
Rev. Martin Luther King Jr.
to unheralded ministers such as
the Rev. Napoleon P. Chapman
(pictured here), the pastor of a
small South Carolina church in
the mid-20th century.*

CONTENTS

AFRICAN-AMERICAN ACHIEVERS

THE HISTORY OF
THE BLACK CHURCH

1

The First African-American Institution

DURING THE 17TH and 18th centuries, the slave trade was one of the most important sources of European wealth. Hundreds of traders made fortunes on the shipment of human beings from the continent of Africa to the Western Hemisphere.

Scholars have attempted to estimate the total number of Africans brought to the Caribbean and the Americas for the slave market, and the numbers vary. Estimates from extended studies by Philip D. Curtin in 1969 put the numbers imported at nine and a half million. These figures do not count the thousands who died in the battles of resistance in their homeland, or those who succumbed to illness, disease, and suicide on the way to North and South America.

Once the Africans were captured, they were dispossessed of their complex culture and familiar social customs. The process of dehumanizing began immediately and was continued consistently until the slaves' arrival in the New World and subsequent purchase by a white owner. Before shipment, prisoners were held in a holding area called a "baracoon," much like what today would be called a concentration camp. They remained there with those of other

A Dutch ship brings African slaves to the English settlement at Jamestown, Virginia, in 1619.

9

tribes and languages until a trader came to purchase them. No regard was shown for tribal differences or family ties. Upon purchase, slaves were crammed into the holds of ships like cargo, with barely enough space to lie down. Often half a ship's human cargo would die en route to the New World.

Those slaves who were shipped to Brazil and the West Indies worked on giant sugar and cotton plantations. This meant little contact between the slaves and their masters, allowing the slaves to maintain some of their old ways. In the North American colonies that eventually became the United States, the situation was different. There were some large plantations that needed slave laborers, but the majority of slaves were purchased by the owners of small plantations or farms. Most owners held less than 20 slaves.

Upon arrival, the new slaves were slowly broken in to plantation work. Resident slaves who were already established in the work routine often took pride in their familiarity and knowledge of the new environment. They pressured newcomers to work hard to acclimate themselves and fit in. These circumstances prevented newcomers from using their former language. In addition, owners strictly forbid their slaves to use their native language.

On a smaller farm, a slave might work side by side with the owners, thereby becoming familiar with all members of the family. Those on the larger plantations were ruled by an overseer. The overseer kept the slaves under close surveillance even when they were in the slave quarters and not working. A common rule prevented more than five slaves from gathering together without the presence of a white person.

It didn't take long for slavery to rob the transplanted Africans of their cultural and social bonds. The close-knit family and tribal associations they'd once enjoyed were destroyed. Familiar customs relating to their work and religion became a vague

memory, as did former systems of kinship and orga-nized social life.

As the South became filled with thousands of slaves, farm owners began buying and selling slaves in much the same way they bought and sold cattle and horses. Slaves' attempts to form immediate fam-ily units were futile, since a spouse or child could be sold at any time and shipped off to another area—perhaps to another state. The continual threat of being purchased away from all that was familiar fur-ther strengthened the dehumanizing process.

Arising out of the deep social void caused by slavery in the United States was what came to be known as the Black Church. The term "Black Church" does not refer to any one institution; instead, it is a collective name for the myriad of Christian churches and denominations African Americans created to worship as they pleased. These

Quakers were members of a religious group originally estab-lished in England by George Fox during the 17th century; seeking freedom to worship as they wished, many moved to the English colonies in North America. The Quakers believed strongly that all men are created equal, and during the 18th and 19th centuries many worked to end slavery.

Cotton Mather, a Puritan minister in colonial America, opposed slavery through his writings.

churches came into being as a joint effort of free blacks and slaves, from both the North and the South—often in the face of great danger, opposition, and persecution.

African Americans in the North fared significantly better than their counterparts in the South. In 1619, a Dutch ship brought over 20 blacks and sold them to European settlers in New England. However, from all records, it appears that the 20 were treated as indentured laborers and were later set free. One among them, Anthony Johnson, became a respected land owner.

The population of free blacks in the Colonies continued to grow throughout the 17th and 18th centuries. This growth was due in part to children born of free blacks, mulatto children of mixed black and white marriages, children of free black and Native American parentage, and also slaves' children who were set free.

In the North, slaves were frequently freed. In fact, by the end of the 18th century, the states north of Delaware had passed legislation emancipating slaves. Because the economy of the North was based on small family farms and trade, rather than on plantations like that of the South, slavery was not an economic necessity. In addition, several religious groups, particularly the Puritans and the Quakers, objected to slavery on moral grounds.

The practice of freeing slaves became an issue for southern slave owners, who did not want the population of free blacks to increase. By the 1830s, in the southern states (first in Maryland and Virginia), legal restrictions were set in place to prevent private owners from freeing slaves.

The Puritans had a strong influence on attitudes toward slavery in the North. In early Colonial days, the Puritan fathers held sway not only in church life, but in the community and in government. These influential leaders held a strong opposition to slavery and often spoke out against the practice. Puritan leader Cotton Mather, in his 1706 tract *The Negro Christianized*, argued vehemently for the humanity of blacks. In it he states:

> One Table of the Ten Commandments, has this for the Sum of it; *Thou Shalt Love thy Neighbour as thy Self*. Man, thy *Negro* is thy *Neighbor*. . . . Yea, if thou dost grant *That God hath made of one Blood, all Nations of men*; he is thy Brother, too.

Although Cotton Mather argued that African slaves should be taught about Christianity, members of the clergy throughout the Colonies soon learned that expressing this idea brought down the wrath of slaveholders. For the most part, slave owners strongly resisted the wholesale conversion of their slaves. They thought that Christianity would make slaves think they were equal to their white owners. Slaveholders feared Christianity would make their slaves not only proud, but rebellious. Rebellious slaves might get the idea they could fight for their freedom and win. Organized insurrection among slaves was the one thing slave owners feared the most.

While some Christian groups spoke of freedom for slaves, it was the Quakers who put action behind their words. As early as the 17th century, Quakers set up religious training for slaves to help them prepare for freedom. Not only did Quakers free their own slaves, but they worked to change the legal restrictions against the private emancipation of slaves. Thus from the earliest days right up until the Civil War, the Quakers became the strongest enemies of the institution of slavery.

Free blacks in Colonial America began forming connections to Christianity decades before southern slaves. Many were affected by what was called

Richard Allen was cofounder of the Free African Society, the first African-American organization in the country. This Philadelphia-based society was rooted in religious principles; it later grew into the African Methodist Episcopal church, one of the largest black religious denominations in the United States.

the Great Awakening. This revival, spearheaded by a preacher named Jonathan Edwards, took place in the 1730s. The revival spread quickly through New England communities, and out of the spiritual awakening several black preachers emerged. At first, black converts and black preachers were welcomed into white churches. In Delaware, a freed black preacher by the name of Richard Allen traveled with white ministers. He was given assignments by Bishop Asbury of the Methodist Church around 1786.

When Allen went to Philadelphia, he saw that his people needed religion. He proposed a separate church for the African Americans there. At first, this was opposed by both blacks and whites. However, opinions changed when several blacks were dragged from where they were praying in St.

George's Methodist Episcopal Church so that whites could be seated. One of those forcibly moved was Allen himself. Allen and several other black leaders then formed the Free African Society in 1788.

Members of the Free African Society began organizing churches. In Philadelphia, Allen's friend Absalom Jones organized the African Protestant Episcopal Church of St. Thomas, while Allen founded the Bethel Church. The old building in which his congregation met was purchased and dedicated in 1794. Allen started as a deacon and later became an elder. Soon the Free African Society movement spread to other cities, where new churches sprang up. The leaders of these churches remained in close contact. In 1816, they met in Philadelphia and established the African Methodist Episcopal (A.M.E.) Church as a denomination. Allen was elected bishop.

Numerous secessions in neighboring New England cities followed suit as blacks broke away from white churches. In 1796, the congregation formed what would later become the African Methodist Episcopal Zion (A.M.E.Z.) Church. Still other, smaller, black denominations came into being, such as those derived from Presbyterian and Congregational churches. Independent black Baptist churches were also established during this time, though they were not as well organized. It would be much later before black Baptists would come together in a national denomination; the National Baptist Convention, U.S.A., was founded in 1895.

Back in the deep South, the spread of Christianity among the slaves was progressing slowly. Most of the missionary work among the plantation slaves came by way of such organizations as the Anglican Society for the Propagation of the Gospel in Foreign Parts. Beginning in 1701, this England-based group emphasized extensive religious instruction, which did not appeal to the slaves.

A handful of free blacks did manage to found organized churches in the South in the 18th century. Between 1733 and 1775, the First African Baptist Church was established on the William Byrd plantation in Mecklenberg, Virginia, and the Bluestone Church established by a slave named George Liele who was converted during the Great Awakening. In 1788, Andrew Bryan organized the First African Church of Savannah, Georgia.

It wasn't until what was called the Second Great Awakening that Christianity began its wildfire sweep throughout the South. This revival, occurring near the end of the 18th century, came about primarily through clergymen of two denominations: the Methodists and the Baptists. Rather than stressing extensive teachings as a prerequisite for salvation, these itinerant preachers emphasized an experience with God. Repentance and a change of heart led the converts into a conversion experience.

The message was simple, clear, and easy to understand. This was a concept the slaves could grasp and hold as their very own. The idea of a personal relationship with Jesus as the Son of God spoke to the slaves' trampled dignity, giving them a renewed sense of self-worth. This heavenly relationship transcended the power of their earthly masters.

Another aspect of the Second Awakening that appealed to African Americans was the exciting camp meetings. Both Baptists and Methodists employed traveling evangelists, or circuit-riding preachers, who traveled throughout the South setting up meetings. These emotional revival meetings might last for several days.

A key aspect of this revival was the music. Along with the fiery sermons, the slaves heard fresh new hymns. These songs, which brought hope to the slaves' dismal lives, were taken back to the cotton fields and the slave quarters, where the slaves transformed them. Some have said they "Africanized" them with different rhythms, chants, and intonations. From the earliest infusion of Christianity among enslaved blacks, music flowed forth. The music was uniquely theirs, and it would become an integral part of worship in the Black Church.

The Methodist leaders of the Second Great Awakening—John Wesley, Francis Asbury, and Thomas Coke—were emphatically against slavery. In a 1780 conference, 17 Methodist clergy voted that all traveling evangelists must free their slaves. They declared that "slavery is contrary to the laws of God, man, and nature—hurtful to society."

After the leaders freed their slaves, the rules were then extended to the members of the Methodist Church. As soon as members of the Methodist Church were told to free their slaves, strong opposition arose. Thomas Coke traveled to Virginia and preached against slavery, after which he was threatened by a mob and served with indictments in two counties. One angry woman promised a reward to anyone who would give Coke 100 lashes. Realizing they had stepped into a volatile and sensitive area, the Methodist leaders reluctantly withdrew their demands. While they still went on record as abhorring the practice, they felt their movement was too young and their numbers too small to actually seek the destruction of slavocracy, the faction of slave owners and advocates of slavery who held such power in the South. In a journal entry dated in 1798, Bishop Asbury admitted that "slavery will exist in Virginia perhaps for ages; there is not a sufficient sense of religion nor of liberty to destroy it. . . ."

The leaders were faced with a difficult dilemma. Was it more important to fight slavery, or to win the souls of the slaves and attempt to minister to them as best they could? They opted for the latter. Those who had once advocated the abolition of slavery now found themselves trying to convince reluctant

A runaway slave attempts to elude pursuers on the opposite bank of the river, while making his way toward the promised land—free northern states or British-controlled territory in Canada. Slave owners attempted to keep Christian missionaries from teaching slaves to read, fearing that religious instruction might make their slaves more rebellious.

slave owners that Christianity would make the blacks better slaves—more docile and more obedient. Preachers and missionaries were forced to prove that Christianity was no threat to slavery. Slaveholders, however, were not easily convinced.

The continued exodus of runaway slaves added to slaveholders' fears. Slave owners offered large rewards for the capture and return of these runaways. Advertisements for runaway slaves filled southern newspapers; many of the advertisements specifically stated that the runaway was a Methodist or Baptist. One such ad appearing in the *Maryland Gazette* on September 4, 1800, spoke of a slave named Jacob who was 35 years old. The ad stated: "He professes to be a Methodist, and has been in the practice of preaching of nights." These ads caused all slave owners to question whether Christianity made their slaves more docile or more rebellious. As slave owners grew wary, southern missionaries found their work among the slaves greatly restricted.

Yet another problem hampered the work of missionaries—the growing strength in the North of vocal, active abolitionists. These were whites and free blacks who printed agitating documents and made bold speeches condemning the practice of slavery, demanding that it be completely abolished. The growing abolitionist fervor served to feed the slaveholders' mistrust of all missionaries. Ironically, the hardworking white missionaries who made the long, arduous treks from plantation to plantation, working diligently among the slave population, came to resent the vocal abolitionists in the North. In order to maintain the favor of slaveholders and access to the slaves, these missionaries began defending slavery as a positive good and emphasizing the purely religious nature of their mission. In 1841, the Missionary Society of the Methodist Conference of South Carolina wrote, "So to preach the Gospel . . . is the great object, and we repeat it, the *sole* object of our ministrations among the blacks."

Slave owners feared that if their slaves could read, trouble would surely ensue if they received abolitionist literature. Therefore, owners demanded that religious instruction be done orally. This method was referred to as a "religion without letters," in which teachers asked questions and students stated answers until all was memorized.

In 1835, the Presbyterian Synod of South Carolina and Georgia trumpeted the success of their strategy of placating slave owners:

> The religious instruction of our slave population, entirely suspended in some parts of the country . . . through the lamentable interference of abolition fanatics[,] has proceeded with almost unabated diligence and steadiness of purpose through the length and breadth of our synod.

The southern churches' strong sentiments against the abolitionists eventually caused deep divisions among the leadership of white denominational organizations. Of course, this represented only one of many areas in which divisions occurred between the North and South in the years leading up to the Civil War.

Regardless of the safeguards slave owners attempted to set in place, slave insurrections and revolts still occurred. One led by an ex-slave named Denmark Vesey in 1822 was elaborate and well planned. Vesey, a respectable carpenter in Charleston, South Carolina, loved liberty and wanted to help blacks still in slavery. He said that he had read his Bible and discovered the truth that

Denmark Vesey, a former slave who had purchased his freedom, later became a minister at a black church in Charleston, South Carolina. Vesey felt that the Bible did not support slavery, and attempted to encourage a slave uprising in the South in the summer of 1822; however, authorities got wind of the plan. The revolt was broken up, and Vesey and other conspirators were hanged on July 2, 1822.

slavery was wrong. For years he plotted a revolt, carefully choosing his assistants and collecting an arsenal of weapons. Word leaked out, however, and the plot was foiled. At least 139 blacks and 4 whites were arrested and imprisoned. Thirty-five blacks, including Vesey, were hanged.

The bloodiest revolt took place in 1831. It was led by a slave named Nat Turner from Southampton County, Virginia. He and his followers killed Turner's master, Joseph Travis, and his family. Within 24 hours, 60 whites had been killed before the slaves were stopped by state and federal troops. Scores of the insurrectionists were killed in the battle; others, including Turner, were later hanged.

Like Vesey, Turner also spoke of being led by God to help set his people free. These revolts and others caused a deepening fear and mistrust of all slaves by their slaveholders. The increased number of revolts, in addition to an ever-increasing number of runaways, compelled slave owners to invoke stronger restrictions on slaves, keeping a closer vigil over them.

By the eve of the Civil War, most slaves, if they were not Christians, had certainly heard the gospel message. Most were familiar with Christianity's doctrines and symbols and its vision of a redeemed life. The slaves' particular mode of worship had been growing and maturing. Some would later refer to the growing slave church as the "invisible institution." Out of mistrust of their masters' preachers, untold thousands of slaves resorted to holding their own meetings in quiet, secluded spots often called "hush harbors." In the secrecy of their quarters, down in a hollow, deep in a thicket, near a river or creek bank, they held their prayer vigils—sometimes all night long.

Later testimony from slaves revealed that they fearlessly risked life and limb to enjoy this private worship. Ex-slave Moses Grandy claimed that slaves were often flogged "if they [were] found singing or praying at home." Another claimed that her "oldest brother was whipped to death for taking part in one of the religious ceremonies."

The slaves had to resort to imaginative ways to maintain secrecy, but this did not deter them. They came to rely on the spiritual refreshment that came from prayer, preaching, song, and communal support to counteract the agonies of day-to-day life. They prayed for deliverance and for freedom, believing strongly that if they did not live to see it, surely their children would.

The slaves' true religion did not reflect that of their masters. Their Christianity was discovered and developed in secret places and meetings. Their religion was their very own, perhaps the only thing they possessed that no one could take from them.

2

After the Civil War

Newly freed blacks at a Union army camp during the Civil War. With the end of the war, and passage of the 13th, 14th, and 15th amendments to the Constitution, nearly 250 years of slavery ended.

IN 1861 THE CIVIL WAR began, born of increasing frustration and conflict between the radically different and deeply divided North and South. On January 1, 1863, in the midst of the conflict, President Abraham Lincoln issued his Emancipation Proclamation, which freed all slaves in the rebellious states. Although the Proclamation's effect would not truly be felt until the war was over, southern slaves were finally beginning to witness the fulfillment of their long-held prayers for freedom.

During the war, many African-American men served in the Union Army. As the southern slaves heard the news that the Civil War was being fought to free them, many fled the plantations and sought refuge behind Union lines. Some who did not leave refused to work and were accused by their owners of insolence, arrogance, and insubordination. Other slaves became informants, guiding the federal troops to strategic places and then aiding them when they arrived at the plantations.

In 1865 the Union victory ended almost 250 years of enslavement and changed the entire fabric

As former slaves began to develop their own communities in the South, the church remained central to black life.

of the nation. That same victory also ushered in new and complex problems as nearly four million people strove to adjust to their newfound freedom. Most African Americans wisely understood that the 13th Amendment to the Constitution, which outlawed slavery, was merely a piece of paper and would not immediately ensure total political and economic freedom.

In the war-ravaged South, thousands of former slaves were displaced, wandering about the countryside hungry and destitute. Those who had lost spouses and children through earlier sales went in search of family members. In the months following the war, African Americans held several conventions to work toward improving their conditions. During these conventions, freed slaves requested fair wages, measures for the relief of suffering, and the abolition of the Black Codes, recently passed laws that restricted the civil rights of ex-slaves.

While their cries fell on deaf ears in the South,

private organizations in the North brought pressure on Congress to send aid for the needy, both black and white, in the South. From this appeal, the Freedmen's Bureau was established. This bureau furnished medical services, established schools, and supervised contracts between freed slaves and their employers.

The bureau made great strides in the area of education. Many teachers came from the North to help set up new schools. These included day schools, Sunday schools, industrial schools, and colleges. In addition to the work of the Freedmen's Bureau, the North's organized black churches also funded and established schools.

It was during this time that the "invisible institution" began to merge with the established institutional church—the free black churches organized before the war. At this time, there was neither sufficient manpower nor money in the organized churches to teach ministers or to create new ministries. Meanwhile, hundreds of freed slaves were converging on southern cities. This mass of humanity was detached, disorganized, and lacking what little stability they'd known in their "slave families" and their "slave churches."

To fill the leadership void, the Black Church commissioned untrained black men who felt "called to preach" and sent them forth to do needed work among the people. The main qualifications were an ability to preach and sing well. The preacher skilled at both was almost certain to be blessed with a large congregation.

What resulted was an explosion of growth in the black churches. In a period of 10 years, between 1856 and 1866, the A.M.E. Church had grown from 20,000 to 75,000. This mushroomed to 200,000 by 1876. The Baptist churches also enjoyed phenomenal growth. Everywhere throughout the South, local black churches were established in communities both large and small. In 1866, the Negro Baptists held their first state convention in North Carolina. Other southern states soon followed suit with their own Baptist conventions.

The merging of more-educated blacks with those fresh off the plantation was not without difficulties. Some leaders opposed the freed slaves' noisy outbursts and emotional singing during services, and sought to curtail them. One bishop in the A.M.E. Church stated that he opposed the singing of spirituals, which he called, "corn field ditties." He further said that the church must drive out such a "heathenish mode of worship." In time, major differences were overcome, allowing the Black Church to become the major source of spiritual and material relief during the rebuilding period after the Civil War called Reconstruction.

It is difficult to grasp fully the vital importance of the institution of the organized church in the lives of blacks during the era between the Civil War and the turn of the 20th century. No longer were there laws to prevent black preachers from preaching or requiring whites to supervise black services. The Black Church was the sole area that belonged completely to African Americans; it became their cultural, social, and political center.

As former slaves sought to piece their lives together in a new world, preachers encouraged them to build strong families by marrying and staying with one spouse—and to remain faithful to that spouse and their children. This teaching was especially important since few slaves had any frame of reference for a normal family life. Under the harsh restrictions of slavery, fathers had been no more than visitors in the family setting, if that. Finally, African Americans had a chance to form stable, two-parent families.

Following Emancipation, black men began to gain some economic authority. The freedman and

his wife and children could rent land and begin to operate their own farm. To rent the land, men were required to sign a lease agreement, which gave them a new sense of responsibility and self-worth. Many of these farmers subsequently rose up as leaders and spokesmen in their local churches.

During Reconstruction, a number of black men were voted into public office in southern states. In South Carolina, the first legislature following the war was made up of 87 blacks and 40 whites. South Carolina also had two black lieutenant governors and two black speakers of the house.

One highly educated black man, Francis L. Cardozo, served as South Carolina's secretary of state from 1868 to 1872 and its treasurer from 1872 to 1876. Having studied at the University of Glasgow and also in London, he was considered "one of the best-educated men in South Carolina, regardless of color." Other states also saw representation of blacks

This Currier & Ives print shows a group of African-American congressmen from the Reconstruction era. Pictured are (front, l-r) Hiram R. Revels of Mississippi; Benjamin S. Turner of Alabama; Josiah T. Walls of Florida; Joseph H. Rainy of South Carolina; R. Brown Eliott of South Carolina; (back) Robert C. DeLarge of South Carolina; and Jefferson H. Long of Georgia. Revels was the first black to serve in the Senate; the others served in the House of Representatives.

in their legislatures, but not in as great a number as South Carolina.

It was not surprising that many of these politicians were pastors of black churches. Hiram R. Revels, a senator from Mississippi, had been an ordained minister in the A.M.E. Church and was also a schoolteacher. Henry M. Turner, also of the A.M.E. Church, helped organize blacks in the Republican Party in Georgia. He was eventually elected to the Georgia legislature and served there until the return of white supremacy forced him out. He was later appointed by President Grant as postmaster of Macon, Georgia. When he was forced from that position, he dedicated the remainder of his life to working within the church. Another A.M.E. Church leader, James W. Hood, was elected president of the first political convention organized by blacks after the war. Hood served both as Deputy Collector of Internal Revenue for the United States and Assistant Superintendent of Public Instruction of the state of North Carolina.

In spite of this seeming political progress, trouble continued to brew just beneath the surface throughout the South. Anger, bitterness, and resentment among whites soon drove them to overthrow Reconstruction efforts and regain power. They did this through a brutal combination of outright harassment and violence and a legislative assault on blacks' civil rights. Those Northerners who worked through branches of the Freedmen's Bureau complained bitterly of the resistance they met from white vigilante groups. Bands of men roamed throughout the South attempting to keep "the Negro in his place." They went by such names as Regulators, Jayhawkers, and the Black Horse Cavalry.

As a further show of strength, whites formed secret societies such as the Knights of the White Camelia, the Pale Faces, the White Brotherhood, and the Knights of the Ku Klux Klan. Of the many

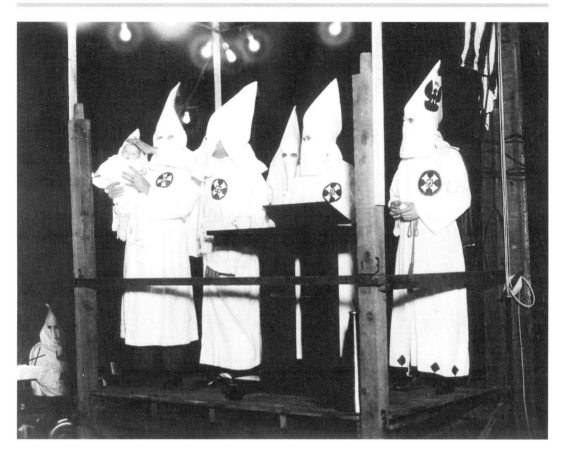

secret societies, the most powerful were the Camelias and the Klan. These groups kept a continual patrol in various parts of the South, brandishing weapons and using intimidation, force, bribery at the polls, arson, and even murder. Their ultimate goal was to deprive the black community of its right to vote.

While Congress made efforts to curtail these activities, for the most part these were unsuccessful. Soon the idea of equal opportunities in the South became a cruel joke. Every type of tactic was used to prevent blacks from casting their votes. Laws were enacted requiring poll taxes and literacy tests, which put voting out of reach for the poor or under-educated—as most ex-slaves were. Polling places were moved and hidden so blacks could not find

Organizations such as the Ku Klux Klan emerged in the South during the 1870s, intending to terrorize freed blacks and deprive them of their rights. Among their tactics were church burning and the lynching of ministers and other black leaders.

them. The most effective deterrent to black voters was the threat of whippings and lynchings as well as having barns, houses, and crops burned.

Throughout the 1870s in the South, the struggle was on for political control of the entire region. Since blacks voted a nearly straight Republican ticket (Lincoln's party was the Republican Party), white employers were urged to hire only Democrat voters. Slowly but surely, the Democrats returned to power, strangling Reconstruction efforts and all but squeezing out any representation of the Republican Party in the South.

After a few years, the North became weary of the crusade to help blacks. Business and industrial interests were more important. Thus neither the black community nor the southern Republican party could expect any help from Congress or the Supreme Court to uphold laws to protect the voting rights of blacks.

In the national elections of 1876, results in South Carolina, Louisiana, and Florida were contested. To break this impasse, the Republicans offered a trade-off: if the southern states allowed the election to go Republican (placing Rutherford B. Hayes in office as president), the party would remove troops from the South and allot federal subsidies for internal improvements. Once in office, Hayes withdrew the troops and removed other restrictions, as promised. This left the South to itself once again to govern as it willed, marking the end of Reconstruction.

In 1883, the Supreme Court outlawed the Civil Rights Acts of 1875, which had been passed to prevent discrimination. Southern legislatures wasted no time passing laws that banned all blacks from white hotels, barber shops, restaurants, and theaters. These were referred to as "Jim Crow" laws. As the states throughout the South adopted new constitutions, segregation laws became even more stringent, requiring separate schools and other public facilities for blacks. The monetary expense of this double system became an enormous economic burden on the entire region.

Little by little the black community saw their political gains slip from their grasp until the promise of economic and social equality could no longer be realized through political means. African Americans realized that one of the few ways to elevate themselves was through education.

From early on, education for blacks was tightly intertwined with their religion. The first educators to teach slaves were, of course, the missionaries. The motivation for learning was to study the Bible and the moral teachings from Scriptures. Learning for the sake of learning was an unfamiliar concept.

During Reconstruction, northern teachers sent by church organizations converged on the South. In addition, many of the black men who graduated from denominational colleges returned to their communities to build schools as well as churches. This dedication was vital since only a fraction of public funds was allotted for the education of black children.

During the age of philanthropy, throughout the 1880s and 1890s, wealthy white families donated money specifically for the education of blacks. The Julius Rosenwald Fund, for example, contributed approximately $4.2 million toward the construction of more than 5,000 schools for black children in the South over a 20-year period. Often, members of the black community also donated toward their own schools. They raised the money through simple measures such as church suppers and other fundraisers. A number of black colleges and universities were built during this era.

Since the white community was more than

White philanthropists such as Julius Rosenwald donated funds to help build schools for African-American children in the South during the late 19th century. However, state spending on education for blacks in poor rural areas lagged far behind school spending on white children.

In 1901, novelist Charles Chesnutt visited his hometown of Wilmington, North Carolina, to study the causes of a recent riot. He summed up the situation this way: "The rights of the Negroes are at a lower ebb than at any time during the thirty-five years of their freedom, and the race prejudice more intense and uncompromising."

happy for blacks to build their own facilities, they did little to stop this area of development. In fact, the conclusion was that if the philanthropists helped to educate blacks, the taxpayers' money would go to educate the whites. The results of this reasoning can be seen in the allotment of public education dollars. By 1900 every southern state had enacted laws that provided for separate schools for blacks and whites, and by 1935 the southern states spent, on average, nearly $38 to educate each white child while spending just $13 per black child.

Eventually, black institutions of higher learning found ways to sustain themselves without public funding. One example is Fisk University, which created a group known as the Jubilee Singers to travel and entertain to raise funds. Their tours included a trip to Europe. Within seven years the Jubilee Singers had raised over $150,000.

In addition to schools, the other area where blacks experienced the most freedom and control was in the church. When African-American politicians were forced out of office after the end of Reconstruction, most returned to their churches, although some became heads of schools and black universities. Within the confines of the church, politics continued on a smaller scale. There African Americans were free to elect leaders and officers and engage in the business activities of the church.

Outside of the family, the church became African Americans' most accessible social group. In both the North and the South, blacks were treated as outsiders in almost all aspects of social life. Therefore, they were intensely loyal to, and dependent upon, their churches and church organizations. What once was called the "invisible institution" now became the "nation within a nation."

Out of the churches grew mutual aid societies designed to assist one another in times of sickness, poverty, and death. Often the very names of the societies reflected their ideals: "Love and Charity," "Builders of the Walls of Jerusalem," "Sons and Daughters of Esther," and "Brothers and Sisters of Charity," for example. Within these mutual-aid organizations grew the seeds of what would later become secular insurance companies. Black banks also began to emerge to grant loans to African Americans for private business ventures.

Fraternal organizations that reflected the hearts and minds of the black community were formed even before the Civil War. The Knights of Liberty had been organized by a preacher named Reverend Moses Dickson, who was an active worker in the Underground Railroad, a network of safe houses set up by abolitionists to aid runaway slaves. Following the war, the Grand United Order of True Reformers was created by Reverend Washington Browne. Begun in Alabama and later moved to Virginia, the True Reformers organized a newspaper, real estate firm, bank, hotel, building and loan association, and grocery store.

Increasingly, the Black Church functioned far beyond the normal requirements of a church body. In addition to being the local forum, literary society, and theater, it became a welfare agency. Various community programs included working in slums and jails, as well as establishing homes for orphans and the aged. In the cities of New York, Detroit, Chicago, and St. Louis, black churches organized homes for working girls, clubs for boys and girls, schools for domestic training, schools of music, and employment agencies.

Unlike their northern counterparts, black churches in the South remained predominately rural. The census of 1890 showed that nine out of ten African Americans lived in the South, and more than 80 percent of those lived in rural areas. In many areas of the South, one preacher often served several churches, alternating between congregations on Sundays. In his absence, lay leaders rose up to fill the void, creating additional leadership opportunities within black society. These rural churches reflected the schedule of their agricultural society, often holding powerful revivals in the fall just after the crops were harvested. These meetings, lasting two to six days, recalled the camp meetings of the Second Great Awakening. Still, these churches had much in common with their urban sisters; they served as community meeting places and reached out to help members in times of need.

As the 19th century came to a close, the rural nature of the Black Church and black life was about to undergo a huge change. Almost en masse, thousands of African Americans began migrating from the rural areas to the cities and from the South to the North. This amazing geographical shift, referred to as the Great Migration, profoundly affected the Black Church.

Several unrelated incidents provoked the Great Migration, not the least of which was increased violence. From 1884 to 1900 more than 2,500 lynchings (mostly of blacks) occurred throughout the South and a few in the Midwest. This barbaric and illegal means of dispensing punishment, in which mobs killed supposed offenders, usually by hanging, continued unchecked for decades. The reason most generally given was that a black man had attacked a white woman. Records show that this was rarely the case. Numerous cases of blacks being beaten, whipped, and burned alive were also reported.

Wholesale crop failures triggered by droughts, leached—or overused—soil, and the cotton-destroying boll weevil precipitated a massive economic crisis. Most blacks worked as sharecroppers after the Civil War, which meant they rented land

and equipment from whites. Their lot in life was little better than when they were slaves, since most white planters disregarded contracts and often failed to pay stipulated wages. When the economic reversals came, sharecroppers suffered the most. When hard times became even harder, blacks began looking for a way to escape.

Another event that further worsened conditions in the South was the Supreme Court's 1896 ruling in the famous case *Plessy v. Ferguson*. The court's decision stated that separate facilities for blacks were legal as long as they were equal. This ruling extended segregation laws to include such things as separate schools, separate hospitals, and separate seating on trains. By 1900, even public water fountains had signs above them stating "Whites Only" and "Colored." Life for most blacks in the South was becoming unbearable.

American novelist Charles Chesnutt visited his hometown of Wilmington, North Carolina, in 1901 to study the causes of a recent riot. He summed up the situation this way: "The rights of the Negroes are at a lower ebb than at any time during the thirty-five years of their freedom, and the race prejudice more intense and uncompromising."

A mass exodus began in the years prior to World War I. Fed up with social and economic hardship and lured by the promise of industrial jobs, thousands of African Americans headed North. Just as freedom from slavery had once represented entry into the promised land, the North had become their new promised land. Hope was born anew.

3

The Great Migration

With the start of World War I, many African Americans moved to the industrial cities of the North, where they could find employment in factories converting to the war effort.

ON JUNE 28, 1914, a Serbian nationalist assassinated Archduke Franz Ferdinand of Austria. Austria declared war on Serbia on July 27, and by the following month Germany had invaded Belgium. All of Europe was suddenly embroiled in a massive war.

While President Woodrow Wilson promised to keep the United States out of the war, the nation certainly felt the effects. The numbers of European immigrants dropped drastically. In addition, many workers of European origin left to return to their homelands and fight. Large northern industrialists were suddenly faced with a severe labor shortage. This left them only one alternative, an alternative they would never have considered before—southern blacks. Thus the Great Migration began in earnest.

In the early days of this historic population shift, industries in the North openly recruited young, single black men as workers. Tobacco growers in Connecticut, for instance, grew alarmed when their Polish, Lithuanian, and Czech workers left to return to Europe. These farmers turned to the National Urban League, a nonprofit organization

The influential educator Booker T. Washington felt that blacks should remain in the South. Other black leaders, such as W. E. B. DuBois, argued that the migration was an effective protest against the disenfranchisement of African Americans in the South.

dedicated to aiding African Americans, for help in recruiting black students from southern schools for seasonal work. The farmers promised free rides on the Pennsylvania and Erie Railroads to the workers. Soon railroads and steel mills followed suit, sending empty train cars to be filled with potential workers.

Some of these early recruits were considered to be "loafers" from the "bottom of the South's labor pool." They lived in camps near the railroad or factory. In this setting, left to themselves, they became involved in drinking, gambling, and fighting, creating a bad name that made life more difficult for many local blacks who had worked hard for years to establish a good reputation. Few, if any, of these newcomers had any interest in developing church ties.

Some churches sized up the situation and stepped in to minister. Reverend William A. Creditt, president of Downington Industrial College, organized Social Uplift meetings at a railroad camp near Philadelphia. However, Creditt's work touched only a few and made but a small impact.

The practice of indiscriminate importing lasted only a few years before black leaders in the North began to protest. Industrialists soon learned it was not in their best interest since these types of workers had high rates of absenteeism. Plus, when promises of better wages and easier work were in sight, these workers walked off the job.

The next wave of migrants consisted of entire families who had been pushed off their land—victims of political and economic repression. Many in this wave were well educated, possessed work skills, and showed good character. These were stalwart church members with no fear of hard work. While some were so poor they had only the clothes on their backs, others were property owners who were willing to leave all and take the risk. The North beckoned to them with hopes not only of higher wages, but of freedom from fear and danger with the promise of new opportunities.

Not all black leaders felt the promises were true. Some, such as the highly educated Booker T. Washington, felt it was outright dangerous for blacks to pin their hopes on such flimsy promises. Washington pointed out that the South was their homeland; their roots were there. He felt they were better suited to be farmers and tillers of the soil than city dwellers.

At the 26th Tuskegee Negro Conference held in 1917, attendees adopted a statement urging blacks to stay on their farms and work in cooperation with sympathetic whites. That same year Reverend Richard D. Stinson, principal of the Atlanta Normal and Industrial Institute, spoke at a camp meeting in

Arlington, Georgia. He stated his shock that migrants had sold farms, livestock, and furniture to move north and start all over. Stinson appealed to the white community to step forth and support industrial education for blacks. "Let the two races treat each other right," Stinson argued, "and there is plenty of room, wealth, and happiness for the white man and the negro in this section."

W. E. B. Du Bois, editor of a black-run magazine called *The Crisis*, totally disagreed. He argued that a mass exodus was the "only effective protest that the Negroes *en masse* can make against lynching and disfranchisement." He chastised southern black leaders for spending more time talking about the virtues of living in the South than they spent protesting lynching and lawlessness.

Meanwhile in Washington, D.C., President Wilson was strangely silent regarding the hundreds of reported lynchings of African Americans. He was blamed for the failure of the Dyer Anti-Lynching Bill, in spite of the fact that all church leaders called out for its passage. At one point a delegation from the bishops' council of the A.M.E. Church met face-to-face with Wilson to protest lynchings, mob violence, Jim Crow laws, and discrimination against African Americans. Their protests went unheeded.

In an ironic twist, the white community in the South, whose poor treatment of blacks was a driving force behind the Great Migration, grew disturbed as they watched badly needed black laborers leaving in droves. In a September 1916 issue of the *Montgomery Advertiser,* white planters were urged to give black tenants free use of land, seeds, and supplies. When such promises did not work, whites turned to threats and intimidation. They asked for laws to prevent the activity of labor agents. In some places, police arrested potential migrants as they were boarding trains heading north. In still other areas, wholesale roundups of blacks took place to

The biblical story of Moses, who led his people out of slavery in Egypt and into a land promised to them by God, was an inspiration to Christian blacks; many compared their northward journey to the Israelites' trek to the promised land.

prevent them from leaving.

While the conflicts raged on, the migration swelled to greater and greater numbers. Upon the United States' entry into World War I in 1917, a great industrial war machine sprang into action, demanding an even greater number of workers. In some parts of the South, entire towns and villages—families along with the pastors, teachers, and storekeepers—left everything and moved northward. From 1914 to 1918, the black population of Detroit, for example, increased from 5,500 to more than 30,000.

Black church leaders attempted to search for deeper meanings in the unprecedented movement of African Americans. Reverend C. M. Tanner of Allen Temple A.M.E. Church in Atlanta referred to it as "The Second Exodus," comparing the blacks' northward trek to the biblical journey undertaken by the enslaved Israelites as Moses led them to the promised land. He believed Scriptures were being fulfilled and the hand of God was at work.

Tanner was not alone. The A.M.E. Ministers' Alliance of Birmingham stated that the great exodus "is God's plan and hand." Still others compared the devastating floods of 1916 and the boll weevil infestations to the plagues that befell the biblical land of Egypt before Moses and the Israelites embarked on their journey.

The North bore many parallels to the biblical promised land. Throughout years of slavocracy, the slaves looked with hope to the North. When abolitionist activists and Underground Railroad conductors such as Harriett Tubman became the slaves' "Moses," the direction to freedom was always north. In addition, north is referred to as "up" and so is heaven. Thus many clergy emphasized not only the search for jobs and good wages, but the search for a new sense of liberation as well.

An interesting aspect of this phenomenon is that it lacked a leader. No one person was responsible for stirring up the black community and urging them to leave the South. No leader existed to make sure the movement was orderly and safe. And no leader existed to ensure that all those who moved north would find a safe haven when they arrived.

Organized black churches and their leaders in the North were greatly confused as to how this influx would affect them and how they were to respond. Many were totally unprepared for the waves of migrants. Dissension occurred among the officers of the organized black denominations in regard to the steps that should be taken.

Some pastors started grandiose building programs. Others purchased existing structures from whites at inflated prices. The folly of these expensive ventures came clear in 1929 when the stock market crashed and the Great Depression began. New buildings, however, were signs of success, and they filled both the clergy and congregation with a sensation of great accomplishments. The extensive growth of these northern churches had little to do with a major spiritual revival. Instead, it was a result of people moving their memberships from the churches in the South to those in the North.

A few of the stronger churches set up plans to help meet the basic needs of the migrants. Reverend Adam Clayton Powell Sr., pastor of Abyssinian Baptist in Harlem, opened a soup kitchen for the hungry migrants. His son, Reverend Adam Clayton Powell Jr., moved the church into welfare work and also assisted black workers in their attempts to strike and form unions for fair wages. (The younger Powell later became the first elected black congressman from New York state.) In Chicago, the Good Shepherd Church sponsored a well-organized community center. Unfortunately, these examples of organized social outreach were few and far between.

An additional problem was the contrast between the southern and northern churches. Churches in the North were larger than what the migrants had been used to in their small, close-knit communities of the South. Northern churches were organized to the point of being cold and bureaucratic. Newcomers missed the warmth and the individual attention they'd received from their pastors. They also missed the strong preaching that warned against sin and presented an almost euphoric emphasis on the glories of heaven. Pastors in the North had learned to preach what their congregations wanted to hear, which amounted to a sort of secular social gospel. Most of all, the migrants missed the opportunities to be demonstrative during the service. They soon learned that emotional participation such as singing and shouting marked them as being from the "lower class." These restrictions led many migrants to start their own churches in small storefront locations.

While northern churches were in a quandary about their mushrooming numbers, the southern churches suffered great losses. A pastor in Savannah, Georgia, Reverend Bolivar Davis, reported that more than 10,000 laborers and mechanics had left the city, and 500 of those were from his church. He then moved to Alabama to preach and reported that "the Northern fever is raging down here." The numbers lost were astronomical. An estimated 5,000 to 8,000 A.M.E. members left South Carolina. The Baptists estimated that in Georgia alone, up to 69,000 members were lost.

Pastors grieved to see their people leave all that was familiar and launch out into the unknown. Many of these leaders who saw the possible dangers awaiting their flocks used the opportunity to call southern whites to repentance. A.M.E. Bishop William D. Chappell of South Carolina openly condemned lynchings, the Ku Klux Klan, and unfair white landlords. At the same time, however, he urged other A.M.E. pastors to discourage the exodus.

Black pastors in the South faced a dilemma of grave proportions. They feared the white authorities' reaction if they spoke in favor of the exodus. If they spoke against it, however, their congregation might accuse them of wanting blacks to remain in bondage. Many parishioners lost trust in their pastors, refusing to confide in them. They just quietly moved away without giving anyone a chance to talk them out of it. Many pastors settled their dilemma by packing up and leaving right along with their congregations.

As if this migration—and controversies about the migration—were not challenge enough, there arose yet another element in the early 20th century that would alter the Black Church. In 1906, out in Los Angeles, an incredible revival took place. This revival, known as the Azusa Street Revival because of its location, continued at a fever pitch for over three years. The black evangelist who led the revival was William Joseph Seymour.

The roots of the Azusa Street Revival began to

develop in 1867, when a white Methodist minister named Charles Parham broke away from the Methodists and opened a Bible school in Houston, Texas. There he taught about a more perfect relationship with Christ, often referred to as a Holiness group or Holiness teaching. A number of African Americans attended Parham's classes in spite of the fact that they were made to sit in the back or outside the classroom. Seymour was one of those who heard Charles Parham's teaching.

Moving to California, Seymour began preaching at the Apostolic Faith Gospel Mission located at 312 Azusa Street. People flocked to hear his messages, and many were reportedly "falling under the spell of the Holy Ghost." Revivals had long been a hallmark of both African-American and white

These African-American soldiers, members of the 369th infantry division, won the French Croix de Guerre for their heroism in battle during World War I. Blacks who fought with distinction returned home from the battlefield to find prejudice and discrimination remained strong.

Repent Ye Therefore And Be Converted That Your Sins May Be Blotted Out When The Time Of Refreshing Shall Come From The Presence Of The Lord. Acts 3-19

For God So Loved The World That He Gave His Only Begotten Son That Whosoever Believeth In Him Shall Perish But Have Everlasting Life. St. 3:16

The rise of Pentecostalism in the early 20th century marked a significant change in the development of the Black Church. After the Azusa Street Revival in Los Angeles in 1906, the Pentecostal movement spread throughout the country. This 1934 photo shows a baptismal service at the Pentecostal Faith Church in Harlem, New York.

congregations, especially in the South and Midwest. Azusa Street, however, was different. Seymour preached that the principal element of becoming "saved, sanctified, and filled with the Holy Ghost" depended on the experience of "speaking in tongues." This was based on the description of the day of Pentecost in Acts 2:4, in which the apostles spoke in languages they did not know as a sign of being filled with the Holy Spirit.

There is no clear record of the number of people who attended the Azusa Street revival, but it is estimated to be above 50,000. From the outset, whites were welcomed and encouraged to attend services. People came from all over the nation, and later, from all over the world. They stood in line for hours just to attend one of the services.

From this event came what was to be known as the Pentecostal or Holiness movement, which spawned a number of African-American Pentecostal and Holiness groups. Every Pentecostal denomination worldwide can trace its roots either directly or indirectly to the exciting events at the Azusa Street Revival. Thus Pentecostalism became the only denomination in the United States that sprang from Black Church origins. It did not remain confined to the United States, but spread rapidly throughout Africa, Asia, and Latin America. The number of Pentecostals around the globe swelled to between 25 and 35 million in the 1970s; by the early 21st century, that number had increased tenfold, to about 350 million Pentecostal Christians worldwide.

An African American from Tennessee by the name of Charles Harrison Mason attended the Azusa Street Revival for five weeks. He received the Baptism in the Holy Ghost and spoke in tongues in March 1907. After returning to Memphis, he started what became known as the Church of God in Christ (COGIC) denomination. COGIC experienced the most amazing growth of any black denomination up to that point. By the 1990s its numbers had reached five million members, ranking second only to the National Baptist Convention.

For many years, COGIC stood as the only incorporated Pentecostal body in existence. It was the only authority to which independent white Pentecostal churches could appeal. Consequently, many white pastors served in COGIC pulpits and were ordained by black pastors.

Charles Parham himself attended the services at Azusa and worked with Seymour for a time. Parham, however, did not advocate the overt demonstrations of emotion present in Seymour's meetings. Eventually, Parham split off from Seymour and started the Assemblies of God in 1914, which resulted in racial division. Ironically, in later years, black Pentecostals were excluded from many of the national Pentecostal organizations.

Bishop Mason (leaders in black COGIC churches held the title of Bishop) showed a remarkable ability to cultivate leadership and delegate responsibility. It was his strategy to send evangelists and bishops into the major industrial cities of the North, which resulted in COGIC becoming a predominately urban church. This practice was known as church planting.

Due to lack of funds, many COGIC churches began in simple storefront facilities. Renting vacant business space, founders would turn it into a place of worship. Typical furnishings might include a pulpit, a Bible, folding chairs, musical instruments such as a tambourine or battered piano, a religious picture or two, and a curtain to divide the sanctuary from the space behind the pulpit platform. Established churches often accused these storefront churches of stealing their church members.

Not all storefront churches were set up by Pentecostals. Baptist and Methodist migrants who longed to reestablish the types of churches they'd had in the South also turned to the more simple trappings of a storefront. In these unpretentious surroundings, African-American worshippers enjoyed their own brand of demonstrative services and sang their own songs.

As extreme changes were taking place in the black community in America, changes were also taking place in the armed forces fighting overseas during World War I. African Americans not only served in World War I, but they became highly decorated, battle-proven soldiers. Black regiments received numerous awards and citations, and hundreds of African Americans sacrificed their lives. In Europe, black soldiers were treated as equals. They moved about freely in France, associating socially with French men and women. General Goybet, commanding officer of the 157th French Division, praised the Negro regiments by stating, "These crack regiments overcame every obstacle with a most complete contempt for danger." Unbiased acceptance was a totally new experience for most of the young black soldiers.

Homecoming for American troops meant parades up Fifth Avenue in New York City with more than a million people crowding the streets to watch. From Boston to Buffalo to Chicago, veterans were hailed as conquering heroes in grand parades. After such a hearty welcome, and after having paid such a high price to help win the war, the returning black soldiers fully expected to move up to a new level of democratic living in the United States. These dreams, however, were quickly dashed.

The years immediately following World War I became the bloodiest yet in the history of America's volatile race relations. Jobs became scarce when industry scaled back at the close of the war. White laborers resented the blacks who, they claimed, were taking all the good jobs. They also resented the fact that blacks now wanted to live in "their" neighborhoods. During the summer of 1919, more than 25 race riots took place. Some were large, some were small, but all were bloody. They took place in the South *and* the North, resulting in millions of dollars of damage to homes and businesses.

Fanning the flames of this unrest was the Ku Klux Klan. This group, numbering more than 100,000, promoted race hatred against Negroes, Japanese, Roman Catholics, Jews, and all foreign-born people. Blacks, however, received the worst of the punishment. During the first year of the postwar period, more than 70 blacks were lynched. Many were flogged and 14 were burned publicly. Many of the victims were still dressed in the military uniforms of which they were so proud.

This spate of ethnic violence had a new element

Churches come in all shapes and sizes, from imposing stone or brick edifices on busy city streets, to sparsely furnished storefront edifices, to simple wood-frame buildings, such as the one shown here. This photo was taken in Natchitoches, Louisiana, in 1940.

that made it different from the violence blacks had previously endured; black men were now arming themselves and fighting back. No longer was this a case of one race tormenting the other and the other cowering in fear. Some felt these bloody confrontations amounted to an all-out war. One African-American poet of the times, Claude McKay, expressed his race's determination to stand up for their rights:

> Like men we'll face the murderous, cowardly pack,
> Pressed to the wall, dying but fighting back!

Many wondered what role the church should play in these chaotic circumstances. Once again, the Black Church felt the heavy weight of responsibility to lead in perilous times. In some areas, African-American leaders met with city leaders to solve problems. Some churches expanded to create and support extensive social outreaches in their communities.

Even before the riots, African Americans were forming secular self-help organizations, such as the National Association for the Advancement of Colored People (NAACP) in 1909 and the National Urban League in 1910. These were founded with help and support from Black Church leaders. Through secular organizations, black clergy were free to influence the political processes of society without raising questions about separation of church and state.

During the first half of the 20th century, as African Americans discovered that the still-prejudiced North was a far cry from the promised land and as life in the South continued its segregated oppressiveness, American blacks continued to turn to the Black Church as a safe haven. Whether in a storefront, a wood-frame building in a rural southern community, or a large brick structure on the corner of a busy urban street, church to African Americans remained one of the few places they felt comfortable.

Novelist Richard Wright, in his book *12 Million Black Voices*, wrote, "It is only when we are within the walls of our churches that we are wholly ourselves, that we keep alive a sense of our personalities in relation to the total world in which we live. . . ."

Throughout the Great Depression and on past the years of World War II, African Americans continued the search to find their place and their true selves. The church continued to be the anchor that held them firm. In the even more tumultuous future, the church would become a lodestar and lighthouse in the darkest hours.

4

The Civil Rights Movement and the Black Church

IN SEPTEMBER 1950, in Topeka, Kansas, a part-time preacher by the name of Oliver Brown was fed up. Since his family lived quite literally on the wrong side of the tracks, his little girl, Linda, had to walk through the railroad switchyard to reach her all-black school a mile away. Another school, located only seven blocks away, was exclusively for white children.

That September, Oliver Brown took Linda, then a third-grader, to the all-white school and attempted to enroll her. When the principal refused to enroll his daughter, Oliver Brown sought help from McKinley Burnett, head of the local branch of the NAACP. Eventually 13 parents filed suit against the Board of Education for equal rights for their children.

The case was taken to the U.S. District Court of the District of Kansas. While the judges there were sympathetic, they felt they could not overrule the *Plessy v. Ferguson* case from 1896, which cre-

Attorneys for Oliver Brown and other parents who had filed a lawsuit against the Board of Education of Topeka, Kansas, discuss the case. Among them is Thurgood Marshall (seated on table), who would go on to become a justice of the U.S. Supreme Court. Brown, a minister, was one of many men and women who helped African Americans in their fight for civil rights during the 1950s and 1960s.

ated "separate but equal" school systems for blacks and whites.

Undeterred, Brown and the NAACP took the case all the way to the Supreme Court. On May 17, 1954, in its famous *Brown v. the Board of Education* decision, the court threw out *Plessy* and declared for the first time that segregation was illegal. The quiet, unassuming, black preacher from America's heartland had changed the course of history.

Oliver Brown was only one of many African Americans who changed American society in the 1950s. In Montgomery, Alabama, on December 1, 1955, a black woman named Rosa Parks was riding the bus home from work. She was seated in the back of the bus, but when a white person came on, the driver ordered Mrs. Parks to give up her seat. (During this time, blacks were not only made to sit in the back, but also were forced to stand if a white person came on and needed a seat.)

Like Oliver Brown, Rosa Parks was fed up. She refused to move. She did not argue. She did not get angry. She just sat there. The police arrived, and Rosa Parks was handcuffed and whisked off to jail.

Such injustices were not new in the South, but seldom had such a thing happened to so prominent a black person. Mrs. Parks had once served as secretary for the Montgomery branch of the NAACP. She was active in the Montgomery Voters League and the NAACP Youth Council, and she was held in high regard by her local African-American community.

Dr. Martin Luther King Jr., pastor of the Dexter Avenue Baptist Church in Montgomery, met with other black leaders to discuss ways to protest the arrest of Mrs. Parks. The answer was a large-scale boycott of the city bus lines. Forty thousand fliers were printed and passed out among the black community to announce the plan. On December 4, black ministers all over the city conveyed the plans for the boycott from their pulpits.

On the first day of the boycott, the bus company suffered a 90 percent loss of revenue. African Americans who usually rode the bus shared rides with friends or walked. Some even rode mules! The white community fought back with terrorism and harassment. Dr. King's home was bombed, as was the home of another black leader, E. D. Nixon. Blacks were arrested for loitering as they waited for rides; black drivers were arrested for picking up hitchhikers. Mrs. Parks received threatening phone calls. But no one in the black community buckled under the pressure.

The boycott lasted nearly a year. On November 13, 1956, the Supreme Court declared that Alabama's state and local laws requiring segregation on buses were illegal. On December 21, 1956, Dr. King and a white pastor, Reverend Glen Smiley, rode together in the front seat of a public bus!

When Rosa Parks refused to give up her seat to a white passenger on a Montgomery, Alabama, bus, she inspired a civil-rights protest. Local ministers encouraged the Montgomery Bus Boycott; among them was a young man who would go on to become a national leader, Dr. Martin Luther King Jr.

The Southern Christian Leadership Conference was a group dedicated to achieving civil rights while adhering to Christian principles. It was founded in 1957, and based at Ebenezer Baptist Church in Atlanta.

Thanks to the relatively new medium of television, the entire country was able to watch the drama unfold. The boycott captured the nation's attention and moved Dr. King into a position of leadership. Using Christian principles he'd learned in church as a child and applying the techniques of nonviolent protest pioneered by Mahatma Gandhi, Dr. King attempted to create an effective way to protest for black rights.

From the outset, the civil rights movement was born within the Black Church. King's deep relationship with the church had tremendous influence on the direction in which he steered the movement. He was the person who gave the Black Church the vision of its power to effect change. This idea of latent power in the hands of the people was a new concept for the black community.

King developed a well-organized and ongoing coalition of leaders who were, first and foremost, leaders in their churches. King first served as head of the Montgomery Improvement Association, and later as founder and head of the Southern Christian Leadership Conference (SCLC). His strategy always centered around Christian principles. His task, as he described it, was to "be militant enough to keep my people aroused to positive action and yet moderate enough to keep this fervor within controllable and Christian bounds."

The SCLC was founded in 1957. Some 60 churchmen, mostly ministers, gathered at Ebenezer Baptist Church in Atlanta, the church pastored by King's father, Martin Luther King Sr. The SCLC served as Martin Luther King Jr.'s base of operation throughout his involvement in the civil rights movement until his death in 1968. The conference called for peaceful, nonviolent methods to make black voices heard. Addressing segregated African Americans, the conference stated that "non-violence is not a symbol of weakness or cowardice, but as Jesus demonstrated, non-violent resistance transforms weakness into strength and breeds courage in the face of danger."

This living, breathing example of Christianity in action was difficult for white churches to ignore. The few white clergymen who supported King's views and cause quickly found themselves without jobs, causing them to choose silence instead. Eventually, however, many white clergy and laymen joined in the movement with their finances, affirmation, and even their physical presence in marches and demonstrations. There were individual cases of whites making incredible sacrifices as they faced the same dangers as blacks. A few even gave their lives.

Dr. King would soon have many enemies—some of whom were leaders in his own denomination. Dr. Joseph H. Jackson, president and leader of the National Baptist Convention, felt King was a menace. It was Jackson's belief that the role of the pastor was to preach the gospel and effect change only by exemplary conduct. These kinds of disagreements led some black pastors to form their own denomination, the Progressive Baptist Alliance, from which stronger and more vocal Black Church leaders arose during this era. King was a key promoter of this change.

One firm supporter of King was Leon Sullivan, pastor of Zion Baptist in Philadelphia. While Sullivan could be proud that in the late 1950s blacks in his city had access to public facilities, he was dismayed that so few blacks had jobs in those facilities. Conducting an intensive study, he found that there were no black salesmen-drivers for soft-drink companies, bakeries, or ice-cream companies. Only a few blacks worked as bank tellers, clerks in supermarkets and stores, or stenographic workers in offices. Sullivan set out to change that situation.

Sullivan, who had served under the tutelage of Adam Clayton Powell Jr. at Abyssinian Baptist in Harlem, organized an alliance of black ministers. Their plan was similar to the Montgomery boycott. They refused to do business with companies that did not hire black workers. They called it "Selective Patronage." This technique soon spread to Atlanta, Detroit, New York, and other cities.

Sullivan took the process a step further and established what were known as Opportunities Industrialization Centers (OIC). These centers were set up to train African Americans to competently fill available jobs. The training emphasized moral commitment by the trainees and taught them black history and self-esteem.

Another economic project, initiated in Sullivan's church in 1962, was called the Philadelphia Community Investment Cooperative. Finances came from church members, who were asked to contribute $10 for 36 months. With these funds they built the Progress Plaza Shopping Center, the first black-owned and -operated shopping complex in the nation.

Through his efforts Sullivan was simply continuing the historical role of the Black Church of contributing to local economic development. Sullivan attributed the success of these projects to "prayer, moral initiative, black unity, and the fostering of an appreciation of money as a prime determinant in human behavior."

Sullivan had based his initiatives on what he'd seen King doing in the South, and his ideas soon spread throughout the country. By 1980, OIC was operating in more than 160 cities, and close to 700,000 people had been trained and placed in jobs. Sullivan went on to become the first African American to sit on the board of directors of General Motors.

Meanwhile, throughout the 1960s, the civil rights movement grew in intensity and conflict. There were lunch counter sit-ins, church kneel-ins, freedom rides on buses to protest segregation of transportation, and marches that turned into mob violence. Any ground gained for equal rights was won in a slow and painstaking manner.

One particularly historic event in the movement was the August 18, 1963, march on Washington, D.C. More than 200,000 demonstrators marched down the National Mall and gathered in front of the Lincoln Memorial. This became the largest civil rights demonstration in the nation's history. The march gave national exposure to the movement and also lent support to the Civil Rights Act, which would be passed the following year.

As the march was being organized, some critics warned that few would attend or that the danger of violence was too great. Organizers A. Philip Randolph and Bayard Rustin ignored the warnings and forged ahead. Surprising even the planners, the turnout for the national demonstration was over-whelming. Blacks were joined by Catholic groups, Jewish groups, the AFL-CIO, civil-rights groups, and scores of church groups. One newspaper reporter wrote, "No one could ever remember an invading army quite as gentle as the two hundred thousand civil rights marchers who occupied Washington."

It was at this gathering that Dr. Martin Luther King Jr. delivered his famous "I Have a Dream" speech. While he called attention to the urgency of the hour in gaining freedom and equality for blacks, he also warned his brothers and sisters to avoid violence.

> Let us not seek to satisfy our thirst for freedom by drinking from the cup of bitterness and hatred. We must forever conduct our struggle on the high plane of dignity and discipline. We must not allow our cre-ative protest to degenerate into physical violence.

To close his speech, he made reference to an old Negro spiritual, "Free at last, free at last; thank God Almighty, we are free at last." This line from the song became the rallying cry for the civil rights movement from that moment on.

While some legislators ignored the demonstra-tion by leaving town, president John F. Kennedy received the leaders warmly. Four months later, Kennedy was assassinated and vice president Lyn-don Johnson became president. Johnson, fully in favor of the Civil Rights Act, helped pass the bill in 1964. It seemed a hollow victory, however, as violence against blacks escalated to alarming pro-portions. There occurred what some called a "white backlash," reflecting many whites' opinion that blacks had pushed too far. Some whites in the North were discovering their own prejudices for the first time.

During the long, hot summer of 1964, bloody riots broke out in the Yorkville section of New York

City and then spread to other parts of the city. Similar disturbances occurred in Rochester, New York; Paterson, New Jersey; Philadelphia, Pennsylvania; and Chicago, Illinois.

Voter registration drives, usually run by local churches, caused stronger opposition than marches. Many southern whites feared that a strong bloc of black voters could change the face of local, state, and even national politics. As voter registration drives took place in the South, the Ku Klux Klan stepped up their activities of terror, which included murders, cross burnings, church burnings, and bombings. Between the years of 1962 and 1965, 93 churches in the South were bombed or burned.

In 1965, the violence came to a head during the historic, bloody Selma-Montgomery protest march in Alabama, in which hundreds of protesters were beaten and jailed. Several were even killed. After television images of police brutalizing the nonviolent protesters shocked the nation, President Johnson sent his proposals for a right-to-vote law to Congress. The bill was quickly passed. This suspended all literacy tests, poll taxes, and other devices that prevented blacks from voting. By the end of 1964, nearly a quarter of a million new black voters had been registered. In that same year, several African Americans won seats in the Georgia legislature as well as in the city councils of several southern cities.

In spite of all of Dr. King's teaching in favor of nonviolent action, many younger African Americans became impatient and restless. For years the Student Nonviolent Coordinating Committee (SNCC, or "Snick") had helped with civil rights

"I have a dream…": Martin Luther King Jr. addresses a crowd of more than 200,000 at the Lincoln Memorial on August 28, 1963.

activities throughout the South. These energetic and idealistic young people felt black leaders were not pressing hard enough. In their minds, equality was still far out of reach. The many injustices they'd witnessed caused anger to simmer. In the summer of 1965, in the Watts area of Los Angeles, the lid blew off.

Fair housing remained an area where there seemed to be no progress in civil rights. States acted to circumvent the new Civil Rights Act by creating their own laws. California reacted with Proposition 14, which blocked the fair housing aspects of the Civil Rights Act. In Los Angeles, more than one-sixth of the city's half-million blacks were crowded into an area four times as congested as the rest of the city. In Watts, as the area was called, anger, despair, and hopelessness prevailed.

On August 11, a routine traffic stop in South Central Los Angeles set off a spark that exploded into a five-day riot. When it was over, 34 were dead, over a thousand injured, 4,000 arrested, and over $40 million in damage was inflicted on property. The commission that later studied the riots learned the violence was not the act of lawless thugs, but rather of ordinary people reacting to poor housing, bad schools, and no jobs.

The idea of fighting back was growing. Many African Americans were impatient with Christian love and nonviolence. The new cry from militants did not demand equal rights within the white government, but rather a takeover allowing blacks to rule. One militant who had moved up through the ranks of the Black Church leadership was James Forman. Forman and other militants formulated what was called the "Black Manifesto," the preamble of which was penned by Forman. In the Manifesto, Forman urged blacks to "think in terms of total control of the United States. Prepare . . . to seize state power."

Soon slogans such as "Black Power" and "Black is Beautiful" were echoing throughout the land. Voices from such African-American leaders as Eldridge Cleaver, Stokely Carmichael, and Bobby Seale dominated the airwaves, drowning out the calm voice of Dr. King. In 1966 a militant group called the Black Panthers was formed. In 1967, the Black Power Conference in Newark, New Jersey, called for the United States to be partitioned into two separate independent nations, one for black Americans, the other for whites. Studies of Africa and African cultures and languages became popular among blacks across the nation. The term *Negro* was opposed as a reflection of slavery. The terms *black* or *African American* were preferred.

Because the church was often the center of social life in African-American communities, whites opposed to civil rights often targeted church buildings for destruction. This 1962 photo shows the smoking ruins of St. Mary Baptist Church in Sasser, Georgia.

The Black Panthers became involved in a number of violent protests in which police officers in Oakland, Cleveland, San Francisco, and New York were killed or wounded. The Panthers' agenda was not entirely violent. They set up health clinics, food giveaway programs, and breakfast programs for black school children. However, their uniforms of black berets, black pants, and black leather jackets, along with plenty of firearms, were a terrifying sight to most Americans.

This militant stance greatly disturbed Black Church leaders. King said, "It is absolutely necessary for the Negro to gain power, but the term Black Power is unfortunate because it tends to give the impression of black nationalism. . . ." On another occasion, he commented, "For five long hours I pleaded with a group to abandon the Black Power slogan." King feared that all the long years of work and sacrifice on the part of the Black Church and their leaders might be lost.

This inner struggle as to how freedom and equality for blacks should be attained became moot on April 4, 1968, when Dr. King was assassinated in Memphis, Tennessee. Although blacks continued to gain civil-rights protection despite the lack of a definitive national leader, further changes would be more subtle.

The power and equality of blacks grew considerably throughout the 1970s. Great strides were made in numbers of black voters. African Americans were elected and appointed to government offices. The black middle class grew in both size and influence. Blacks appeared in greater numbers in sports, entertainment, literature, the marketplace, and the corporate world. The number of African Americans attending college grew from 100,000 in 1960 to 450,000 in 1970. The civil rights revolution ushered blacks into places they barely dreamed of only two decades earlier.

The Black Church suffered from the inclusion of blacks into the white community. Integration, in its many forms, meant African Americans were moving to the suburbs and attending the large white churches. Some left the church altogether, feeling that it reflected the painful past and thinking it was an unnecessary entity in these new and better times.

Thus the "mother" that had created the good times was now discarded and left by the wayside. However, this condition proved to be temporary.

5

Leaders in the Black Church

THE BLACK CHURCH has been blessed with talented, courageous men and women who made it a strong, vibrant institution. Traditionally, men filled leadership roles within the church, and women were relegated to the background. This often-criticized attitude has not prevented African-American women from contributing to and shaping their churches.

FEMALE LEADERS

> Then that little man in black there, he says women can't have as much rights as men, because Christ wasn't a woman! Where did your Christ come from? Where did your Christ come from? From God and a woman! Man had nothing to do with Him.

These words were spoken by the famous Underground Railroad conductor, Sojourner Truth. Addressing a women's rights convention in Akron, Ohio, in 1851, she shed light on the gender wars in the Black Church. Due to the struggles fought by all blacks for racial equality, the problem of sexual inequality within the race was often ignored. All of the seven mainstream black denominations—African Methodist Episcopal, African Methodist Episcopal Zion, Christian Methodist Episcopal, the

Sojourner Truth was a former slave who became a well-known evangelist and spoke for the abolition of slavery and for women's rights during the 19th century.

National Baptist Convention, the National Baptist Convention of America, the Progressive National Baptist Convention, and the Church of God in Christ—have a history of a predominately female membership, but predominately male leadership. In this aspect, black women were twice discriminated against as they attempted to take leadership positions within the church.

Historically, in African culture, women served as priestesses, queens, midwives, diviners, and herbalists. In a number of tribes, the role of the woman in religious affairs was as validated and crucial as that of men. Marriage revealed yet another area of female dominance, as the husband came into the wife's family rather than the other way around.

The slave culture brought on severe changes in gender relationships. The concept of the role of preacher and pastor in the Black Church came mainly from the white churches, where men played the predominant roles of leadership. While it is supposed that some slave women did fill the role of preacher, few recorded examples exist. Because of the absence of any other opportunity for a close-knit, organized society, church leadership became a coveted position. The church was the only area in which black men could find an identity in a racist society. The men did not want to share that accomplishment with female counterparts. Thus, from early on, women were not allowed to be ordained. In some cases, they were not allowed to speak from the pulpit at all.

During the slave years, black women became strategic leaders in the abolitionist movement. Women such as Harriet Tubman and Sojourner Truth not only led many groups of slaves out of the South, they also were noted speakers. Sojourner Truth (born Isabella Baumfree in Ulster County, New York) was said to be able to match the wit and eloquence of freed slave Frederick Douglass, a noted orator. In Sojourner's classic speech "Ain't I a Woman?" quoted from earlier, she spoke out against the neglect of the plight of black women.

As early as 1783, the restrictions on ordination were challenged by courageous women who felt they were as capable as men to fill the pulpit. Although a few succeeded, they remained in the minority. One such pioneer was Amanda Berry Smith, who between 1871 and 1878 became known as a powerful itinerant preacher. A gifted singer, preacher, evangelist, and missionary, she paved the way for other black women. They in turn founded independent storefront churches during the Great Migration. Smith later preached in other countries such as England and India, where she was openly accepted.

With the doors to ordained ministry positions closed, gifted black women turned to other roles within the church, such as evangelists, missionaries, deaconesses, Sunday School teachers, musicians, choir members, secretaries, directors for vacation Bible schools, and hostesses for church dinners. W. E. B. Du Bois once stated that women did "the larger part of the benevolent work" in African-American churches.

At the turn of the century, female leaders from the independent black churches created strong secular organizations, such as the National Association of Colored Women and the Colored Young Women's Christian Association. Nannie H. Burroughs, a leader in the Baptist Convention, established the Woman's Convention Auxiliary to the National Baptist Convention. Still others were activists in the women's suffrage—or right-to-vote—movement. These secular groups were never totally separated from the church. Extensive overlapping occurred in both membership and leadership. Such organizations were powerful forces for social change in northern cities during the Great Migration era, and numerous black women played a part.

The daughter of former slaves, Mary McCleod Bethune (1875–1955) was a Southern educator; she founded a school for black girls in 1904, and formed the National Council of Negro Women in 1935. Bethune later became a special advisor to President Franklin D. Roosevelt.

Many black women made contributions as schoolteachers, for teaching was considered a respectable occupation for women. Mary McCleod Bethune, born in 1875, became a teacher and then founded the Daytona Normal School (later to become Bethune-Cookman College). Dr. Bethune also founded and served as president of the National Council of Negro Women. She was a close friend of Eleanor Roosevelt, and she became the highest-ranking black person in the Federal government by serving on the National Youth Administration and as the director of the Division of Negro Affairs.

Dorothy Height, who became involved with Bethune's National Council of Negro Women, went on to become director of the African American YWCA in Washington, D.C., and a staff member at the National Board of the YWCA. In 1957, Height became president of the National Council of Negro Women, making her one of the most influential African-American women to date. Had the clergy been an option, there's little doubt Dr. Bethune, Dorothy Height, and others like them would have become able ministers. Instead, the Black Church lost them and their talents to secular organizations.

Still, many women won positions of respect within the church. Nearly every Black Church claimed its very own "church mother." This was usually the wife of the founder, or one of the older and more respected women. This position has no counterpart in any white church. In her book *Reviving the Spirit*, Beverly Hall Lawrence calls this personage "Big Mama." Quoting a woman in her church named Patricia Wright, Lawrence writes, "We knew if things were really bad or if something really hurt bad, if you got to Big Mama, she'd touch you, she'd 'lay hands' on you, and you knew it was going to be all right." In some instances, pastors consulted the church mother before making key decisions, demonstrating her influence within the group.

Rosa Parks was a staunch member of her local church, and she came to be known as the "mother of the civil rights movement." Her leadership stand during the Montgomery bus boycott was not an easy one. Not only did she spend time in jail, but she also received many ugly threats and constant phone calls. Under the awful pressure, her husband suffered a nervous breakdown. Throughout the year of the bus boycott, Parks was supported by black church women in the group who provided the boycott's strong foundation, the Women's Political Council in Montgomery. Eventually Parks and her family moved to Detroit, and she became a well-known speaker for the civil rights cause.

Music has served as another primary avenue for black women to attain broad areas of leadership and visibility. African-American female musicians made history throughout the Golden Age of gospel music. Some emerged as instrumentalists, others as singers within vocal groups or as solo acts. Mahalia Jackson, for example, became known worldwide in the 1940s and 1950s as an accomplished gospel singer.

Because traditional African religions permitted women to assume leadership roles, it was only natural for black women to seek leading roles in the Christian church. Despite the obstacles placed in their paths, there are proportionately more black women preachers per church membership numbers than white female preachers. Many African-American women, however, avoided the battle for the pulpit by seeking leadership wherever they could. They fulfilled their responsibilities with persistence, skill, and dignity, and provided hours of self-sacrificing dedication.

MALE LEADERS

For generations, whether slave or free, the black community revered their black preachers and ministers. These men held positions of authority and respect, a privilege they could experience nowhere else. Doors to employment, politics, entertainment, sports, and most other social areas were closed in white-dominated communities. Early in America's history, free African-American pastors of the Black Church became well-known figures and leaders of large congregations. Some even achieved political and social success.

In a brief window of time during Reconstruction, many black men were voted into office. The majority of these were preachers. In 1870, an A.M.E. clergyman, Reverend Hiram Revels of Mississippi, became the first black senator elected to Congress. However, once Federal troops were removed from the South and Jim Crow laws were instituted, voting rights were lost and that window of opportunity slammed shut. Once again, the church became the only venue for politics in the black community.

In this setting, the people voted for their own leaders and practiced democracy on a smaller scale. While in the white man's world an African-American man might be called "boy," in the pulpit of a black church, he commanded attention and respect. In both the North and South, black congregations expected their preachers to provide social as well as religious leadership and to be outspoken about important issues. Thus the pastor became the spokesman for both the good news of the gospel and strong protests against inequality.

During the mid-1920s, when records and phonograph players became enormously popular, the voices of black preachers began thundering in the homes of the faithful, as a number of black preachers produced recorded sermons. The effects of the sermons' messages were multiplied many times over with repeated listenings, and the voices on the records became household names.

It's not clear why recording companies first ventured into recording sermons; however, to their pleasant surprise, a great number became big sellers. In 1925, Columbia became the first company to record sermons. They recorded 10 sermons by Calvin P. Dixon and nicknamed him the Black Billy Sunday (after a famous white evangelist by the name of Billy Sunday).

Of all the pastors who recorded sermons in the next three or four decades, none was better known than a Baptist preacher from Atlanta, John M. Gates. Beginning with a few stiff, self-conscious studio recordings in 1926, Gates was soon producing a more "live" sound that appealed to listeners. Because music interacts closely with preaching in most black churches, he included singing on the recordings. By the end of 1926, Gates had recorded 84 tracks. One Kansas City pastor, Reverend J. C. Burnett, recorded a sermon entitled "The Downfall of Nebuchadnezzar" that sold more than 80,000 copies.

In the 1950s the Rev. Leon Sullivan (shown in a contemparary photo with Coretta Scott King) organized a boycott of companies that did not hire black workers. The "selective patronage" technique soon spread to other cities.

Sermon records could still be found in record company catalogs long after World War II. There's no question that the messages of these black preachers touched the lives of hundreds of people who might never have entered a church, spreading the influence of the Black Church into the homes of nonchurchgoing African Americans.

Reverend Adam Clayton Powell Jr. of the Abyssinian Baptist Church in Harlem took a more political tack to effect change. In the 1930s, he organized the Greater New York Coordinating Committee. Through the work of his 8,000-member congregation and this Committee, he actively fought against job discrimination, using methods similar to Leon Sullivan in Philadelphia. Powell's work ultimately broke the power that New York's infamously corrupt "Tammany Hall" political organization wielded over Harlem. In 1944, he became the first black politician from the East to serve in Congress. Eventually, he became the chairman of the House Committee on Education and Labor.

During the civil rights movement, hundreds of black clergymen led the cause at great risk, the most visible of which was Dr. Martin Luther King Jr. King's grandfather was a founder of the Atlanta chapter of the NAACP, and his father firmly believed in using the church to effect social change. Although King never sought public office, he visited the White House when Kennedy was in office and again during the Johnson era.

After King had won world acclaim, including the Nobel Peace Prize, he was besieged with dozens of offers of pastorates from large northern white churches. He chose to remain where he was, however, feeling that he could do the most good as a leader of the Black Church.

A more active politician than King was his assistant and close friend, Reverend Jesse Jackson. Reverend Jackson, who was standing near King at the moment when King was assassinated, has played a major role in movements for empowerment, peace, civil rights, gender equality, and economic and social justice. In 1984, his campaign for the presidency won 3.5 million votes and registered over a million new voters. Four years later, his candidacy won seven million votes and registered two million new voters.

As a highly respected world leader, Jackson has acted as an international diplomat in sensitive situations, such as negotiating the release of American hostages during the Persian Gulf crisis in the 1990s. In the area of labor relations, Reverend Jackson has worked with unions to organize workers and mediate labor disputes. He is best known for

The Rev. Jesse Jackson remains a high-profile African-American leader. Here, he speaks at Chestnut Street Baptist Church in Louisville during the 1984 presidential campaign.

visiting thousands of schools and encouraging young people to stay off drugs and in school.

Reverend Jackson's People United to Save Humanity (Operation PUSH) negotiated with American corporations and firms to open up franchise possibilities and employment for blacks. True to the church roots from which it grew, the organization never held general meetings on Sunday so as not to interfere with Sunday worship in the Black Church.

Another active politician who has his roots in the Black Church is present-day Oklahoma Congressman J. C. (Julius Caesar) Watts. Watts grew up in Eufaula, Oklahoma, where his father, Julius Caesar "Buddy" Watts Sr., served as part-time pastor of a small black church. J. C. Watts' uncle, Wade Watts, also served as a pastor and worked for many years as a leader in the NAACP. Reverend Wade Watts marched through Alabama alongside Martin Luther King, and his Baptist church in McAlester, Oklahoma, was once burned down by the Ku Klux Klan.

An ordained Baptist pastor, J. C. Watts served for several years as a youth pastor in an all-white church in Del City, Oklahoma. After switching from the Democratic Party to the nearly all-white Republican Party, he became one of the few black Republican politicians elected to national office. In November 1998, Watts was voted in as chairman of the House Republican Conference. This office is the fourth-highest position on the House ladder.

Recent years have seen a severe lack of black male leaders rising up within the churches. In fact, there has been an absence of black males everywhere within the church. This is due in part to severe cultural changes in the inner cities, such as low employment, gang membership, drug culture, and high prison population, all of which keep men out of church buildings. Unemployment causes men to leave their families to look for jobs, forcing mothers to rear their children alone. Gang membership, which stresses bravado and fighting prowess, often views church as a place for sissies and old women. Involvement in gangs nearly always leads to a life of crime.

Statistics have shown that, in proportion to the total population, the number of African Americans in prisons in the United States is extremely high. In 1984, New York State's rate of locking up blacks was one and one-half times greater than that of South Africa, a country historically noted for its mistreatment of blacks under its system of apartheid. Imprisonment rates in the South were also higher than those in South Africa.

One other problem contributing to the dearth of new black leadership is the upward mobilization of the middle-class black community. As successful African Americans move to the suburbs, social contact between blacks in different economic groups has gradually disappeared.

This is not to say that nothing is being done to combat these complex dilemmas in the black community. On the contrary, several churches have resorted to aggressive tactics. Pastors such as the late Reverend Obadiah T. Dempsey of Harlem and his colleague Reverend Wyatt T. Walker of Harlem's Canaan Baptist Church developed drug rehabilitation and counseling programs within their churches. Dempsey was nicknamed the "pistol packing preacher" due to his habit of carrying a gun in response to the many death threats he received during his personal antidrug efforts.

In Washington, D.C., Reverend Henry Gregory

Clergy and activists march arm-in-arm to mark the 33rd anniversary of the 1963 March on Washington. From left are the Rev. Al Sharpton, the Rev. Wyatt T. Walker, Dr. Calvin B. Marshall, and Dick Gregory.

of the Shiloh Baptist Church developed the Family Life Center, which offers programs for black youth and families. With additional grant money, the Family Life Center sponsored the Male Youth Enhancement Program. Using sports to hook young men, the program then offers help in academic areas. The church sponsors math and science tutorial programs, hoping to encourage black youth to consider careers in these fields.

In Chicago, a consortium of 10 churches developed Project IMAGE to strengthen the perception of black males in families, churches, schools, and communities. Likewise, the University of Virginia developed a program called Black Manhood Training: Body, Mind, and Soul. The program is being used in several southern black churches to train deacons in youth counseling.

These and other church projects and programs involve entire families and community groups. Their goal is to ensure that the next generation of black males will provide the strong, able leaders needed for the future. Statistics show that black male teens who remain in church have a better chance of escaping from the ghetto. Within the Black Church, these young men hear messages from the pulpit that encourage pride and self-help. Church-taught young men come in contact with role models of successfully employed adults, both men and women.

While black pastors have often come under criticism through the years for being strong-handed and dictatorial, they have been indispensable to the growth and survival of the Black Church. Dr. Leon Sullivan put it this way:

> Although [the black preacher] has been criticized . . . for what has been called lack of leadership in the colored community, the fact is that without the influence he has exerted through his church, we black people would never have come as far as we have. . . . Every movement of significant proportions to survive in the black community has had its roots in the colored church. . . .

The Black Church has seen many men and women willing to take the helm in a wide variety of areas, from politics, to music, to social and community service. Some have laid down their lives as a result of taking on leadership roles. It is due in part to their dedication and sacrifice that the Black Church has remained strong throughout its history.

6

The Role of Music in the Black Church

IN THE TRADITIONS of African tribal culture, music and religion were inseparable. Physical involvement, such as dancing, singing, and drumming, was integral to worship and allowed every person to take part. Among some tribes the drums themselves demanded honor. Worshippers bowed down to the drums and offered sacrifices to them. Tribal songs had complex melodies, rhythm, and organization. The sounds of foot-stomping and hand-clapping further added to the intricate rhythms of the drums and rattles.

The singing skills Africans developed were not confined to religious worship, but were also used in work songs and lullabies. Dance, too, existed outside worship, as tribal members danced for recreational and social purposes. As with all other aspects of their culture, Africans' music was stripped away when the slaves arrived in the New World.

Still, whites could not completely eliminate these African traditions. From the earliest records of slaves who were converted to Christianity, their

The members of a Harlem church enjoy the music of its youth choir in June 1953. Music has always been an important part of the Christian experience for African Americans.

emphasis on rhythmic preaching, singing, moving, and dancing remains consistent. These modes of worship were quite repugnant to white preachers. Reverend Morgan Godwin, a minister in York County, Virginia, in 1665 wrote, ". . . nothing is more barbarous and contrary to Christianity, than their . . . *Idolatrous Dances*, and *Revels*; in which they usually spend the *Sunday*. . . ."

Two centuries later the story remained the same. In 1845 Sir Charles Lyell commented on the way Christian slaves danced: "Of dancing and music, the Negroes are passionately fond. On the Hopeton plantation violins have been silenced by the Methodist missionaries."

It was during the Second Great Awakening, when hundreds of slaves were converted to Christianity, that the slaves began their own clandestine worship services. Far from the eyes of white owners and over-seers, they created a type of music that belonged only to them. In 1819, Methodist writer John Watson complained about their musical behavior.

> The coloured people get together, and sing for hours together, short scraps of disjointed affirmations, pledges, or prayers, lengthened out with long repeti-tious *choruses*. These are all sung in the merry chorus-manner of the southern harvest field. . . . With every word so sung, they have a sinking of one or other leg of the body alternately; producing an audible sound of the feet at every step. . . . [T]he evil is only occa-sionally condemned. . . .

Other plantation missionaries spoke of the "ring shout," in which the slaves formed a circle and danced, clapped, sang, and rocked their bodies rhythmically. While the missionaries attempted to preach and teach against such actions, they were helpless to stop them.

Ring shouts obviously had roots in the musical tribal culture of Africa. However, it's clear that most slaves used these actions to express genuine emotions of joy and thanksgiving regarding their new Christian experience. From the ring shouts came what was referred to as "running sperichils" (spirituals). Styles of spirituals ranged from the excited tempo of rhythmic dance to the slow, drawn-out songs expressing sorrow and sadness at the misery of the life of a slave.

The lyrics and melodies of the spirituals consisted of a mixture of Bible stories and Christian hymns, and the finished product belonged uniquely to the black slaves. The complex songs amazed those who heard them and puzzled those who attempted to actually write the music. Melodies had only a few tones and were laden with blue (or flatted) notes. This later became the basic elements in music called "the blues," which is still popular today.

The music was also characterized by call and response, syncopation, slides from one note to another, and repetition. Prayers and sermons were presented in a sing-song fashion peculiar to black worship.

The spirituals were improvised on the spur of the moment, so they fit the specific daily experiences of the slaves. One slave noted that when his master unfairly administered 100 lashes on his back, his fellow slaves sang about it that night in the praise meeting. One person's joy or sorrow belonged to the entire group through the use of call and response singing.

Call and response singing is also referred to as hymn-lining, which originated with the Puritans in the American colonies. Since there were not enough hymnbooks for everyone, the preacher would intone a line or couplet from *The Bay Psalm Book* (the first Colonial songbook). In response, the congregation sang the same words after him. In 1707, Dr. Isaac Watts's hymnbook *Hymns and Spiritual Songs* brought a new liveliness to sacred

Call and response singing is common during worship services; the minister first intones a lyric, and the congregation then sings the lyric in response.

music. Blacks heard Watts's songs when they were sung at the camp meetings during the Second Great Awakening.

Whether in the ring shout, in running spirituals, or in hymn-lining, the slaves used songs to express praise to the Christian God. These Negro spirituals would eventually shape the entire style of African-American music.

Some have claimed that, as the Civil War drew near and daring attempts at escape from slavery multiplied, the spirituals carried coded messages. This was partially true. "Canaan Land" and "the Promised Land" could mean either the North or freedom from slavery through other means. The term "steal away" in the spiritual song "Steal Away to Jesus" was used by Harriet Tubman as a signal for slaves who intended to join her in an escape attempt.

Coding, however, was not the sole purpose of the songs. The slaves used the songs to express their identification with their new religion, drawing parallels between themselves and numerous Bible characters and Bible verses.

Following the war, a more formal style of hymn-lining became prominent in the Black Church. As the freed slaves converged on the churches of educated blacks, their spontaneous style of worship was looked upon with disdain. Spirituals were discouraged since they were reminiscent of cotton fields, forced labor, and slavery. The hymns from Dr. Watts' 18th-century hymnbook, borrowed from the white culture (which freedmen longed to imitate), were deemed more acceptable. Still, despite the conflicts between the worship styles of educated blacks and former slaves, music in general and singing in particular remained a vital part of all black churches, large and small, rural and urban, throughout the post-Civil War era.

Performing sacred music outside of the church became a new phenomenon in the late 1800s as quartet singing caught on. What is commonly known as barber shop quartet singing among whites actually originated in the black community. As early as the mid-1850s, African Americans were singing in four-part harmony in informal groups. The more formal organizations came into vogue with the African-American university jubilee singing groups.

Fisk University in Nashville pioneered this concept out of dire necessity. When the university faced bankruptcy, the treasurer and choirmaster, George L. White, took a group of his best singers on a local tour in 1871 to raise money. Meeting with a measure of success, they went on the road, spending three months in the northern states and coming

An 1875 poster of the Fisk Jubilee Singers. The group was formed to help their financially strapped university raise funds; they soon became very popular, touring throughout the United States and abroad.

home with more than $20,000. Later the group traveled overseas as well. Eventually, the Fisk quartets were separated from choir groups, which resulted in there being jubilee singing groups and jubilee quartets. The popularity of both types of groups caught on and quickly spread to other universities, thus allowing church music (or gospel music) performed in a concert setting to become a form of entertainment.

At the turn of the century, vaudeville minstrel shows became popular. In these shows, white actors appeared in skits with blackened faces and were called "darkies." However, many of these traveling companies, due to audience demand, featured black jubilee singing groups. These groups popularized such songs as "Oh Dem Golden Slippers."

The single most important event that changed music in the Black Church in the 20th century was the Azusa Street Revival in Los Angeles. The excitement and emotional fervor present in that revival could not help but spill over into the music. As members of the congregation received the Baptism with the Holy Spirit, they celebrated the victory with improvised songs. None of the standard hymns were sufficient to express the joy and elation present in these meetings.

Songs composed under the spirit anointing usually consisted of one or two lines of poetry, a melody of only three or four tones, and blues-influenced harmonies. None of the soloists leading the music had formal musical training. They sang out of a pure joy of heart; they sang with abandon and passion; they sang with all the power and conviction of the singers of Negro spirituals a century earlier. Quite unintentionally, they created a unique style of singing.

In spite of protest and ridicule from existing Baptist and Methodist churches, Pentecostal groups separated from those denominations and created a new service style—including the fresh new music. The three-year Azusa Street revival drew attendees from every corner of the country. All of these revivalists took this new style of music back home with them. In spite of their initial ridicule, Baptists and Methodists would later include in their hymnals many of the new songs born in this era.

Charles Mason, who founded COGIC, the Pentecostal Church of God in Christ, was not a musician, but he understood the need for music in a service. He encouraged each member to take a turn leading the songs. This resulted in the development of a number of excellent singers. The Pentecostal movement spawned traveling evangelists, singers, and musicians, similar to the Fisk Jubilee Singers. Although these traveling quartets and musicians performed in concerts, audiences were encouraged to feel like a congregation and act as though they were in church.

One difference between the Pentecostal musicians and other black groups and quartets was their use of instruments. While most quartets sang *a cappella* (without accompaniment), Pentecostal groups used percussion instruments and banjos, eventually adding pianos.

A blind woman from Texas by the name of Arizona Dranes became known as one of the first gospel pianists. Dranes, an excellent singer and a gifted pianist, went on to record several albums. Between 1926 and 1928 she recorded over 30 songs for the Okeh Record label and became a celebrated gospel artist. What she brought to the style became known as the "gospel beat." In later years she served as a song leader for Samuel M. Crouch Jr., a pastor in Los Angeles. Crouch's nephew, André Crouch, became known as one of the influential musicians in the religious revival of the 1960s known as the Charismatic Renewal.

In the years following the Azusa Revival, the new term "gospel music" was informally used. However, it wasn't until the songbook *Gospel Pearls* was published in 1921 that the term became official. This new songbook was formulated by a number of noted musicians from the African-American Baptist churches, showing that the Baptists formally recognized the power and majesty of this new music.

The Baptist group who compiled the songbook called themselves *gospel singers*; however, they were much more sedate than musicians such as Arizona Dranes. This new Baptist rendition of gospel music captured the ecstasy of the Pentecostal songs but left off the excess. The book became immensely popular. With the endorsement of the large membership of the National Baptist Convention, *Gospel Pearls* took the new music across denominational lines for all Christians to use and enjoy.

Radio played a major part in spreading black gospel music to all parts of the nation and into every home. By 1926, the Eva Jessye Choir, a choral group from New York, was singing formal arrangements of spirituals on a syndicated radio show. The Utica Jubilee Quartet from Mississippi moved to New York in 1926 to perform on a regular half-hour program on NBC. This program consisted of spirituals, jubilee songs, hymns, and a few secular pieces thrown in for good measure. Soon many other African-American musicians joined their ranks as the popularity of gospel music grew.

By the time the Great Depression had its grip on the land, quartet and gospel music was entrenched solidly on the airwaves. While the depression hurt the record market, there were still many live broadcasts of gospel music that reached hundreds of thousands of listeners of all races. Radio allowed black gospel singing to move from a regional genre to a popular entertainment medium.

While Jim Crow laws could render African Americans helpless in many areas, the regulations had no power on the airwaves. The dissolution of the color barrier sometimes extended into the recording studios, where whites and blacks shared microphones and time slots. There was little or no pay for radio appearances in those days. In fact, some musicians had to pay out of their own pockets for the slots or find sponsors to pay. Most were dedicated Christians who wanted to affect the lives of others with their music.

The most well-known gospel singer, the world-renowned Mahalia Jackson, discovered gospel music at an early age. As a child, she attended a local Baptist church with her family. However, just a few doors from her house was a Holiness, or Pentecostal, church, which Mahalia called "Sanctified." Unlike the Baptist church, which held one mid-week service on Wednesday nights, the Pentecostal church in Jackson's neighborhood met two or three evenings a week in services that lasted late into the

In the 1940s and 1950s, gospel singer Mahalia Jackson made her mark on the music world.

night. In her autobiography *Movin' on Up*, Jackson described these services:

> Those people had no choir and no organ. They used the drum, the cymbal, the tambourine, and the steel triangle. Everybody in there sang and stomped their feet and sang with their whole bodies. They had a beat, a powerful beat, a rhythm we held on to from slavery days, and their music was so strong and expressive it used to bring tears to my eyes.

In addition to soaking up the sounds and rhythms from the Sanctified church, Mahalia spent hours listening to recordings of popular blues singers. By the time she turned 15, she had already formed her style.

The success of her records in the late 1940s garnered her a weekly network radio show. She became the first gospel singer to host and star in her own CBS radio program, launched in 1954. That same year, Columbia Records signed a contract with Jackson and dubbed her the "World's Greatest Gospel Singer."

Eventually, Jackson performed in Carnegie Hall, starred on the Ed Sullivan Show, and sang at one of the inaugural parties for President John F. Kennedy in 1960. In 1963, she sang just prior to Martin Luther King's presentation of the "I Have a Dream" speech, and five years later she sang at his funeral. Mahalia sang all over the world, often before royalty, and always sang the sacred church songs which she had loved since childhood.

Another gospel great was musician Thomas Andrew Dorsey from Georgia, a pianist who felt "called" to serve the Lord with his music. However, unlike Mahalia Jackson, he strayed from that path. During the 1920s he wound up playing the blues (which the church looked upon as the devil's music) in Chicago. When he experienced what he called a second conversion, he renounced secular music and became a full-time gospel musician. From there Dorsey opened a publishing house for the exclusive sale of gospel music by African-American composers. He also helped organize the National Convention of Gospel Choirs and Choruses, Inc. He went on to write so many gospel songs that at times during the 1940s all gospel songs were simply called "Dorsey." His most famous, "Take My Hand, Precious Lord," has been translated into 40 different languages.

Gospel music experienced its heyday in the 1940s, as stations all over the nation—none of which were black-owned—featured black gospel artists. WLAC of Nashville, covering 38 states and reaching eight million listeners, played easy listening in the daytime and gospel in the evenings. WLAC became *the* black radio station for the United States.

During the expansion of gospel music, its parent, the Pentecostal churches, progressed as well. Beginning in shabby storefront churches with a few untrained singers in threadbare robes, they moved up to well-established brick edifices, blazing bright choir robes, huge Steinway grand pianos, and Hammond organs. Acceptance by mainstream Christianity, however, came slowly. In the 1950s, COGIC was called a cult by the National Council of Churches and refused membership. It wasn't until 15 years later—when COGIC numbered 8,000 churches—that the National Council at last accepted it as a full-fledged Christian denomination.

Glitz and glamour, fame and fortune, which a few gospel musicians attained, was the exception and not the rule. Many gospel singers and musicians who chose to travel with the gospel message suffered hardships and problems. In the days before superhighways, travel was precarious at best. Auto breakdowns, extremes of weather, and lack of money were only the beginning. When a black group arrived in a town, there was the problem of seeking "colored" restaurants and hotels or rooming houses. Staying in a rooming house meant several musicians shared a room. Some slept in beds, some in chairs, and some on the floor.

When possible, groups worked through a church network that arranged for traveling musicians to stay in the homes of local church members. To avoid embarrassing moments in a restaurant, musicians simply stocked up at a grocery store and ate in their cars. Despite the hardships along the way—which often included not getting paid—these gospel groups felt compelled to carry on their own personal style of missionary work.

The impact of black church music on contemporary popular musicians has been immeasurable. Almost all black musicians can point to their childhood years and tell how they were shaped and

molded by the music they heard in church.

In the summers between 1945 and 1949 a young woman named Della Reese toured with Mahalia Jackson. Reese, who had been singing in church since age six, also sang with a well-known Detroit female group known as the Meditation Singers. Many have said that the Meditations influenced the Motown Sound of the 1960s and early 1970s, made famous by groups such as the Supremes and the Temptations. One member of the Meditations notes that in their early days "a young fan named Diana Ross" was seated in the front row at many of their concerts. Both Della Reese and Diana Ross later made their marks in the world of secular entertainment.

Ray Charles, Aretha Franklin, and James Brown created "soul" music by borrowing the emotional content and style of gospel music and applying it to secular topics. Ray Charles and James Brown were

Gospel music has had a strong influence on the popular music styles of such performers as Aretha Franklin and James Brown.

both reared in black Baptist churches. Aretha Franklin's father, Clarence LaVaughn Franklin, was pastor of the Bethlehem Baptist Church in Detroit. Reverend Franklin was known for singing his sermons, a style that Aretha mimicked in her singing. The popular 1950s singer Sam Cooke switched from gospel singing to secular, as did Lou Rawls and Brook Benton.

The music born in the Black Church would take yet another turn in the 1960s, where it came to play a vital role in the civil rights movement. Whether sung at a sit-in, at a freedom march, or during the freedom rides, freedom songs drew groups together and bonded them as one unit, bolstering courage in those who might become fainthearted. Demonstrators facing snarling dogs, fire hoses, billy clubs, and bullets leaned heavily on the encouragement provided by communal singing.

Many of the freedom songs were created by changing words in existing songs. For instance, "If You Miss Me from Praying Down Here," was changed to "If You Miss Me from the Back of the Bus." "This Little Light of Mine," became "This Little Light of Freedom." Not all the freedom songs, however, arose from existing music; some were written expressly for the events by established songwriters. Sam Block of Greenwood, Mississippi, wrote the song "Freedom Is a Constant Dying," which was reminiscent of the sorrow songs of the Negro spirituals.

In addition to hiring professional writers to pen the songs, professional musicians took the freedom songs to the stages and concert halls of America. The Freedom Singers, affiliated with the Student Nonviolent Coordinating Committee (SNCC), gained a national reputation as they traveled around the country to raise money for the civil rights movement.

Martin Luther King Jr. said this about the freedom songs:

In a sense the freedom songs are the soul of the
movement. They are more than just incantations of
clever phrases . . . ; they are as old as the history of
the Negro in America. . . . We sing these freedom
songs today for the same reason the slaves sang them,
because we too are in bondage and the songs add
hope to our determination that "we shall overcome."

From the traditions of Africa, to slave quarters
on the plantations, to formal and informal Black
Church services, to civil rights demonstrations, and
to the entertainment media, the music born and
bred in the Black Church touches Americans everywhere. Some have gone so far as to say that black
religious music has been "the primary root of all
music born in the United States," be it blues, rag-
time, jazz, rock 'n' roll, soul, rap, or gospel!

7

Coming Home

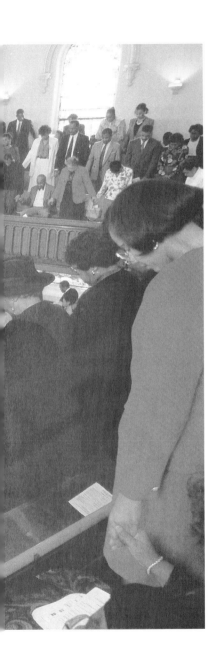

A REMARKABLE phenomenon in the 1990s was the return of thousands of young blacks, both men and women—many educated professionals—to the folds of the historic black churches.

The young professional blacks of the 21st century may not have taken part in a lunch counter sit-in. They aren't too sure who Rosa Parks was. The freedoms they enjoy as middle-class, and even upper-class, citizens have come to them more easily than any privileges their parents and grandparents might have enjoyed.

For the majority, leaving the nest in the 1970s also meant leaving the familiar churches and the traditions and neighborhoods they knew as children. The upward mobility, however, turned out to be a somewhat lonely journey. Not all middle- and upper-class African Americans have experienced the joy and fulfillment they thought should have accompanied their economic achievements. What was missing? For some, it turned out to be the warmth and security of their homey black churches.

In her book *Reviving the Spirit*, Beverly Hall Lawrence quotes Pam Shaw, a member of A.M.E.

The church remains important in the lives of many African Americans.

oric Dexter Street
Baptist Church still stands as
a reminder of the church's role
in the civil rights movement of
the 1950s and 1960s.

Bethel in Baltimore, Maryland, as saying, "Not
going to church didn't work. Going to white
churches or integrated churches, we've been losing
something. . . . We're really disconnected and want
to be connected again. . . . Coming to church is the
most familiar thing in my life now. I can't miss two
Sundays. I start slipping."

Big Bethel, as the old Baltimore church is lov-
ingly called, traces its history all the way back to
1785 and has seen immense changes in the black
community through the years. During the 1970s,

the pews were nearly empty, with only a few hundred active members. In an amazing turnaround, during the 1990s it has ranked among the top five fastest-growing congregations in the nation—white or black. Attendance numbers skyrocketed from around 310 in 1975 to nearly 10,000 by the mid-1990s. Parishioners drive long distances to attend, arriving early to get a good seat. All of these statistics speak of amazing and interesting changes.

For the most part, the historic black churches had remained whole, healthy institutions even when their numbers dwindled. In spite of the downturns of the 1970s, the seven major black denominations never suffered declines as severe as those that occurred in white Christian denominations. A study in the 1980s showed that more than 75 percent of all blacks claimed church membership, and they tended to have higher rates of church attendance than white Protestants. Even as the problems of flagging attendance continued, black churches remained steady and firm. The return of African Americans to their churches proves that all along, their foundations were strong, sound, and secure.

Big Bethel represents a microcosm of recent Black Church growth throughout the nation. The growth is not in numbers alone, but also in spirituality. The new members are intelligent, well-educated persons seeking to know more about God and their daily relationship to Him and with Him. These middle-class members are intensely involved in their churches, whether it be in Bible studies, prayer meetings, and adult education, or politics, activism, and community service.

Another interviewee in Lawrence's book, Sandra Harley Adams, president of her own public relations firm, felt that before coming to Big Bethel she'd been living as a "counterfeit Christian." After a painful breakup with the man she loved, she accepted an invitation from a friend to visit Bethel.

She says, "I think when you're black, when you're in pain, there are three things that you call upon: your mother, your father, and Jesus Christ." At this black church, she found the comfort and fellowship she needed as well as the spiritual resources to help heal her inner pain.

Another reason for the burgeoning numbers is a direct result of the Charismatic Renewal which occurred in the late 1960s and early 1970s. Referred to as a neo-Pentecostal movement, the Charismatic Renewal paralleled Azusa in that emphasis was placed on receiving Baptism with the Holy Spirit and speaking in tongues. The difference in the neo-Pentecostalism of today is that it combines intellect with emotionalism. Pentecostals of the past often disdained education, feeling that worldly education would serve to taint pure religion. Today's Pentecostals can point to scholarly, highly educated leaders, and yet the emotion remains in their open mode of worship where all members take part.

There has long been an underlying difference of opinion among denominations regarding participatory worship. This includes dance, raised hands, verbal "amens" during the preaching, and spirited praise and worship services. Some have felt that more-conservative African Methodism attempted to kill off spontaneity with empty rituals. On the other hand, the more organized churches accused the upstarts in the Pentecostal churches of being too wild and out of control. In the final analysis, it appears to be the enthusiastic worship services that draw blacks back to the churches by the thousands.

"Music is the lifeblood of a soulful worship service," writes Lawrence. "Bethelites like a joyful noise. Singing is second only to preaching as a magnet for attracting new members, and it is the primary vehicle for spiritually transporting the entire congregation."

The Charismatic or Pentecostal influence has

resulted in both spiritual revitalization and enormous church growth, infusing energy and excitement into churches that have lain dormant for decades. This healthy growth is spawning fresh new leaders and swelling the numbers of those attending Bible colleges and divinity schools. Big Bethel, for example, once had more than 50 assistant ministers-in-training simultaneously serving at the church.

The growth explosion has also meant the infusion of new funds, allowing for amazing economic opportunities. A great number of black churches are choosing to channel this money into community outreach programs in a number of ways. Big Bethel established a private Christian school, operates a soup kitchen for the poor, and has become actively involved in local politics. The church provides a forum for officials and candidates. Ward A.M.E. in Los Angeles sponsors a prison ministry. This program involves church members in Bible studies and prayer sessions with inmates. The in-prison ministry has expanded to include a halfway house, and it also supplies assistance to the families of inmates. Payne Chapel A.M.E. in Nashville set up health fairs to give their members free medical screening and advice.

On an even larger scale, First A.M.E. church in Los Angeles moved quickly into the leadership vacuum left by city-wide riots in 1992, caused when a jury failed to convict white police officers who were videotaped beating black motorist Rodney King. The church, known as FAME, became an "economic lifeline" to its South Central neighborhoods. Its Micro Loan Program, funded by church money and two large grants, loans thousands of dollars to

The Rev. Calvin Butts, head of the Abyssinian Baptist Church of Harlem, is one of many Black Church leaders striving to make a difference in the lives of members of their congregations.

small business entrepreneurs in the area. All loan recipients are aided by a mentor who helps support the business and educate the business owners.

In the Jamaica neighborhood of Queens, one of New York's five boroughs, Allen A.M.E., pastored by Floyd Flake, aims to change the neighborhood. The church runs a housing corporation, which purchased nine dilapidated stores and turned them into a profitable shopping center. Allen Plaza, as it is called, also boasts a home for seniors and a $2 million Christian school for kindergarten through eighth grade.

Similarly, Philadelphia's largest Pentecostal church, Deliverance Evangelistic Church, created Hope Plaza Shopping Center. Opening in 1986, it redeveloped a distressed neighborhood. Deliverance's pastor and chairman of Hope Plaza, Inc., Reverend Benjamin Smith, says, "You can't convince people their only need is spiritual when they are suffering financially. This is an effort to provide some jobs for our young people." Hope Plaza remains a highly successful venture that has not only created hundreds of jobs, but also helped increase property values in the area. New low-cost housing projects are being built in the area, and the run-down parts of the neighborhood are being cleaned up.

In the 1960s the diverse elements of the civil rights movement were cradled solidly in the Black Church; the same is true of this current movement to aid the black community. Educated leaders are learning that the power of ownership and entrepreneurship allows them vast opportunities to make a difference in the lives of blacks nationwide. It's this sense of empowerment that seems to be fueling these vast changes—a sense that the Black Church is no longer a victim, but rather is actively doing good for its own people.

Where once African Americans were forced

into segregated worship, now their options are open. Many choose to come home to the place where they can enjoy and feel comfortable with their "black-ness." Says Lawrence, "In spirit and in truth, the black churches are watering holes for black culture, and just by their presence in the heart of the black community they signal those of us looking to anchor ourselves in the swells of blackness. If only for a day."

While the Black Church has never been, and will never be, a perfect entity providing perfect solutions, it has demonstrated hundreds of years of staying power. It has survived while "under siege for close to four hundred years," as C. Eric Lincoln wrote in his book *The Black Church in the African American Experience*. Black author E. Franklin Frazier refers to the Black Church as a "refuge in a hostile white world." And Lincoln also writes, "Past tradition has cast the Black Church as the proverbial 'rock in a weary land'—the first and last sure refuge of those who call it home, and all those who live in the shadow of its promises."

Whether a watering hole, a lighthouse, an anchor, a refuge, or a rock in a weary land, the Black Church shows no sign of shutting down, pulling back, or changing course today. The institution that has performed such a historic role in the past looks forward to the 21st century with anticipation, excitement, and courage.

CHRONOLOGY

1540–1808	Approximately 9 million Africans are brought from their homeland to North and South America as slaves, first by the Spanish and Portuguese and later by the English and others.
1701	Anglican Society for the Propagation of the Gospel in Foreign Parts begins to send missionaries from England to work among plantation slaves in the South.
1726–1750	A revival called the Great Awakening sweeps through New England. Led by preacher Jonathan Edwards, the revival splits the Congregational Church of New England and converts nearly 25 percent of all colonists—both blacks and whites—to Christianity.
1780	Methodist Conference votes that all traveling evangelists must free their slaves.
1788–1791	Black Methodist preacher Richard Allen incorporates the Free African Society.
1794	Richard Allen separates from white church and organizes Bethel Church in Philadelphia.
1790–1830	Second major spiritual revival in America, called the Second Great Awakening. Methodist and Baptist circuit-riding preachers carry the message from plantation to plantation and hold lively camp meetings. Thousands of slaves are converted to Christianity. The slaves transform messages and songs to their own use in clandestine church meetings. The Black Church becomes the "invisible institution."
1822	Ex-slave Denmark Vesey plans a slave uprising in Charleston, South Carolina, but can not carry out his plan. He and other plotters are arrested, convicted, and hanged.
1831	Bloody revolt led by slave Nat Turner results in the murder of 60 whites. Turner and 16 of his followers are hanged.
1800–1861	Era of Negro spirituals. Following conversion to Christianity during the Second Great Awakening, slaves extemporaneously compose hundreds of songs.
1857	The Supreme Court hands down the decision in *Scott v. Sanford* stating that slaves are not citizens and therefore cannot sue for their freedom.

1863	On January 1, the Emancipation Proclamation marks the beginning of the end of 250 years of slavery in the United States.
1865–1875	During the post-Civil War period known as Reconstruction, federal troops and the newly formed Freedmen's Bureau are active in the South to keep order and help protect the rights of blacks. Many pastors of black churches voted into political office.
1871	Fisk University Jubilee Singers (Nashville) go on their first concert tour.
1876	President Rutherford Hayes orders troops out of the South, ending Reconstruction; Jim Crow laws passed.
1883	The Supreme Court outlaws the Civil Rights Act of 1875.
1884–1900	Heightened violence against African Americans in the South. Over 2,500 lynchings take place, mostly of blacks.
1896	Supreme Court upholds "separate but equal" segregation in the *Plessy v. Ferguson* case.
1906–1909	Azusa Street Revival, led by black pastor William Seymour, is attended by thousands of blacks and whites. Marked by Baptism with the Holy Spirit and speaking in tongues. A new type of music—gospel music—grows out of the revival.
1909	W. E. B. Du Bois helps found the National Association for the Advancement of Colored People (NAACP).
1914–1930s	The Great Migration of African Americans from Southern rural areas into the Northern cities takes place; hundreds of small black churches set up in urban storefront facilities.
1919	Bloody race riots occur in major cities during "Red Summer."
1921	*Gospel Pearls* songbook published by African-American Baptists using music and songs from the Pentecostal church movement. Term *gospel music* becomes established.
1925	Calvin P. Dixon becomes first black pastor to record a sermon.
1940s	Gospel music reaches a peak of popularity on radio stations throughout the nation. Called the Golden Age of Gospel.

CHRONOLOGY

1951–1954	Part-time preacher Oliver Brown files suit against the Kansas Board of Education demanding equal rights in education. Supreme Court overturns *Plessy v. Ferguson* in *Brown v. Board of Education*, declaring segregation illegal.
1955–1956	After Rosa Parks's refusal to give up her seat on a bus, the Montgomery bus boycott begins. Bus boycott thrusts Dr. Martin Luther King Jr. into leadership position and launches the civil rights movement.
1957	Southern Christian Leadership Conference founded; King becomes the leader.
1962–1965	Ninety-three churches in the South are burned or bombed.
1963	March on Washington, D.C., becomes largest civil-rights demonstration in history. King delivers "I Have a Dream" speech.
1964	President Lyndon Johnson signs Civil Rights Act.
1965	Congress passes right-to-vote law.
1965	Five-day riot in Watts area of Los Angeles.
1966	Black Panthers are formed. They advocate force and violence, in direct opposition to the Black Church leaders of the civil rights movement.
1968	King is assassinated by James Earl Ray.
1970s	Integration causes Black Church attendance to dwindle.
1971	Reverend Jesse Jackson breaks from SCLC to form People United to Save Humanity (PUSH). Organization quickly grows to 70 chapters totaling 80,000 members.
1984 and 1988	Reverend Jesse Jackson runs for president on the Democratic ticket, placing emphasis on voter registration.
1990s	Black Churches experience incredible growth in numbers as middle-class, young African Americans make the decision to return.
1998	Ordained Baptist pastor J. C. Watts is voted chairman of the House Republican Conference.

Boyer, Horace Clarence. *How Sweet the Sound: The Golden Age of Gospel*. Washington, D.C.: Elliott and Clark Publishing, 1995.

Durham, Montrew. *Mahalia Jackson: Young Gospel Singer*. New York: Aladdin Paperbacks, 1995.

Franklin, John Hope, and Alfred A. Moss, Jr. *From Slavery to Freedom*. New York: McGraw Hill, 1988.

Frazier, E. Franklin. *The Negro Church in America*. New York: Schoken Books, 1974.

Jakoubek, Robert E. *Martin Luther King, Jr.* Philadelphia: Chelsea House Publishers, 1989.

Lawrence, Beverly Hall. *Reviving The Spirit: A Generation of African Americans Goes Home to Church*. New York: Grove Press, 1996.

Lincoln, C. Eric. *The Black Church in the African American Experience*. London: Duke University Press, 1990.

―――. *The Black Church Since Frazier*. New York: Schoken Books, 1974.

Katz, William Loren. *Breaking the Chains: African-American Slave Resistance*. New York: Atheneum, 1990.

Kent, Deborah. *African-Americans in the Thirteen Colonies*. New York: Children's Press, 1996.

Marshall, Frady. *Jesse: The Life and Pilgrimage of Jesse Jackson*. New York: Random House, 1996.

McKissack, Patricia, and Fredrick L. McKissack. *Rebels Against Slavery: American Slave Revolts*. Losgotos, Calif.: Polaris Press Paperbacks, 1999.

Parks, Rosa. *Dear Mrs. Parks: A Dialogue With Today's Youth*. New York: Lee and Low Books, 1996.

Raboteau, Albert J. *Slave Religion: The "Invisible Institution" in the Antebellum South*. Oxford: Oxford University Press, 1978.

Rappaport, Doreen. *Escape From Slavery: Five Journeys to Freedom*. New York: HarperCollins, 1999.

FURTHER READING

Rennert, Rick, ed. *Civil Rights Leaders*. Philadelphia: Chelsea House Publishers, 1993.

Rogers, James T. *The Antislavery Movement*. New York: Facts on File, 1994.

Rubel, David. *Fannie Lou Hamer: From Sharecropping to Politics*. Englewood Cliffs, N.J.: Silver Burdett Press, 1990.

Sernett, Milton C. *Bound for the Promised Land: African American Religion and the Great Migration*. London: Duke University Press, 1997.

Silverman, Jerry. *Just Listen to This Song I'm Singing: African American History through Song*. Brookfield, Conn.: Millbrook Press, 1996.

Silverman, Jerry. *Slave Songs (Traditional Black Music)*. Philadelphia: Chelsea House Publishers, 1993.

Young, Alan. *Woke Me up This Morning: Black Gospel Singers and the Gospel Life*. Jackson: University of Mississippi, 1997.

INDEX

NORMA JEAN LUTZ, who lives in Tulsa, Oklahoma, has been writing professionally since 1977. She is the author of more than 250 short stories and articles as well as 39 books—fiction and nonfiction. Of all the writing she does, she most enjoys writing children's books.

PICTURE CREDITS